U. S. Grant

and the

American
Military Tradition

Bruce Catton

U. S. Grant
and the
American
Military Tradition

Edited by Oscar Handlin

Little, Brown and Company · *Boston*

LIBRARY OF CONGRESS CATALOG CARD NO. 54–6860

ISBN 0-673-39327-5

H G

HAL

PRINTED IN THE UNITED STATES OF AMERICA

To
Ione Catton

Editor's Preface

THROUGH almost the whole of their history Americans have shown a deep distrust of the military man. The constitutional structure of the United States was explicit in subordinating military to civilian authority, and deeply rooted, popular suspicions have resisted the creation of a military caste with special privileges.

Mistrust of the professional soldier was already evident in the colonial period; the Revolution found mercenaries and regular troops arrayed against the forces of democracy and independence; and, in the nineteenth and twentieth centuries, the reactionary role of standing armies in Europe seemed a clear warning to America. The result was a fixed reluctance to elect military figures to popular office.

From time to time generals like Washington and Jackson were chosen to high office. But these were not professional military men; they were civilians whose titles were acquired in the emergency service of their country. On the other hand, the true professional soldier, whatever honors were accorded him as such, rarely stood successfully for civilian office.

With a few outstanding exceptions! In the aftermath of long, destructive conflicts great military figures were summoned to lead in peace as they had in war. Both the nature of the call and the nature of the response are significant. To understand this is to understand much of the American past.

Ulysses S. Grant was a man superbly fitted by character and background for his role as military leader. He moved unsteadily into the nation's highest office in the period of confusion and great change after the Civil War. But as a civilian the very qualities that made him a great soldier proved a liability. His career thus throws light on a large section of American history. It may also, by analogy, illuminate some of the problems of a later postwar era, which in 1953 again saw a general enter the White House.

OSCAR HANDLIN

Contents

U. S. Grant

and the

American
Military Tradition

I

End of the Golden Age

1. *A Basis for Union*

ALWAYS the human tide flowed west. It had swept over the brim of the Alleghenies years ago, and now there were no more barriers. Mad Anthony Wayne had broken the power of the red men at Fallen Timbers, and that cruel menace was drifting away like the misty wood smoke that dissolved across the growing clearings. Young Oliver Hazard Perry had smashed Britain's fresh-water fleet, and as the shot-weighted hammocks went dropping down the clear green depths of Lake Erie, British control of the interior went down with them. All of the Northwest was safe and open.

Beyond, running past the sunset, the mysterious Louisiana country lay waiting, securely American, threaded by dim trails of wonder and peril. The people could go anywhere they chose, quite literally anywhere: all the way to the undiscovered mountains and the deserts, beyond these to the extreme limit of the imagination. Men could very likely do anything on earth they had the courage to dream of doing.

There was then, in the early nineteenth century, a brief

golden age, like nothing ever known before or since: the
time of it measured in decades, its final effects beyond all
measurement, putting a mark on a continent and on generations of people and on the abiding dreams a nation
would live by. Freedom had become a commonplace of ev-
eryday life rather than a talked-about abstraction, and it
was for everybody. Moreover, it carried its own compul-
sions. Men who could do everything they chose to do presently believed that they must do everything they could.
The brightest chance men ever had must be exploited to
the hilt. And the sum of innumerable individual freedoms
strangely became an overpowering community of interest.

This community of interest extended in many directions
and included many things, but first of all it was a common
insistence on uninterrupted growth and development.

The log cabin beside which a sturdy family wrested
from the stubborn earth everything that it ate, wore or
used was romantic only at a great distance. To the people
who lived there, the life meant hard work and privation,
endurable only if it speedily led to something better and
easier. Freedom had to mean something more than just
the freedom to create a series of isolated backwoods slums,
and regional self-sufficiency was the last thing anyone
wanted. The promise of the new land could be realized
only through a society that turned potential wealth into
cash in hand for everybody.

The people of this brief golden age were gross material-
ists and lofty idealists at the same time. They never imagined that there might be a difference between economic
freedom and political freedom. The two went together,
opposite sides of one coin; like liberty and union in the
oration, they were one and inseparable. All that mattered

was a fair chance to get them. Today was better than yesterday and tomorrow would be better than today. All horizons were open to those who exploited every possibility to the utmost.

At bottom, this came down to a matter of good markets and ready access to them. That meant thinking in terms of the whole country, for this great interior could not be walled in. If men were to live here they must submit to its terms, and its destiny was continental. There must be a national road across the mountains, then canals to connect the lakes with the great rivers and the ocean, steamboats on those waters, railroads when railroad time came. These were not merely desirable: they were in the highest degree essential, for the values which the bright new land offered could be realized only if growth and development were continuous.

So there was a strange transvaluation of values. Pursuing immediate self-interest, the settler developed a profound feeling of belonging to a limitless national community. He believed in progress because he saw progress all about him — less grinding toil for this generation than for the last one, greater freedom of opportunity, a better place to live, finer things to do with one's leisure. The progress was both spiritual and material, and it took place simply because America was different, because in America men could do better by themselves than they had ever been able to do before.

As the land was opened, more and more people came to live in it. They came through the Buffalo and Pittsburgh gateways by the thousands. The "Ohio fever" became a legend, and they brought lifetime savings and household goods with them, to say nothing of immeasurable hopes and shining dreams. Because so many of them came, and because there seemed no limit at all to what men might want and get, this human tide pulled the national center of gravity along with it and helped to shape the future.

The people who lived then were never fanciful enough to say that they were living in a golden age. They had their full share of troubles and miseries and individual problems; and anyway a golden age can be identified only after it has ended. The one thing that is really clear about the men of that time is that they would react with unshirted violence and fathomless energy against anything that limited their ability to grow and expand and exploit the riches of their environment.

Against anything, that is, which threatened the unity and the continuity of the American experiment.

Specifically, they would see in an attempt to dissolve the Federal Union a wanton laying of hands on everything that made life worth living. Such a fission was a crime against nature; the eternal Federal Union was both a condition of their material prosperity and a mystic symbol that went beyond life and all of life's values. Men who had grown up to look upon the Federal government as a very handy and entirely indispensable instrument which they could use in their own self-interest would not even try to understand how other men could see in that same union an unendurable menace.

Nobody had to reason any of this out. When the challenge came the response was instinctive. During the first half of the nineteenth century the Middle West produced a generation that could find in the simple word "union" a thing worth making war for, worth dying for; a generation of terrible fighters, with here and there men who would know just how to lead them.

As one of this fateful generation, there was a child born in a cottage overlooking the Ohio River, at the Ohio hamlet of Point Pleasant, on April 27, 1822. He was christened Hiram Ulysses Grant.

2. *Boyhood by the Ohio*

Jesse Grant was on his way up, and he was just the man for it. Born in Pennsylvania and reared in Ohio, he was essentially a Yankee, both by ancestry and by natural aptitude. It sometimes appears that he was the exact opposite of his son Ulysses. Jesse was talkative, boastful, argumentative, buzzing about constantly with febrile Yankee shrewdness, gifted with a knack for making money. He was the sort to prosper in a new country; aggressive and ambitious, determined to get ahead and having enough native ingenuity and energy to make his wish good.

His Connecticut father, a veteran of the Revolution, had moved to the Western Reserve in northern Ohio around 1800, and he had farmed without prospering. When his wife died he let his family fall apart, moving to Kentucky with his two youngest children and leaving the others, Jesse among them, to be brought up by neighbors.

Jesse fared well enough in this scramble. He "boarded around" on different farms, doing chores in return for his keep, spent two happy years with the family of George Tod at Youngstown, got a very small amount of schooling, and at sixteen set out to learn the tanner's trade — a good trade on the frontier, with its insatiable demand for leather goods. Finishing his apprenticeship, he determined to work as a journeyman just long enough to save money so that he could go into business for himself. For a year or more he lived with his employer, Owen Brown, whose fifteen-year-old son was even then a brooding fanatic on the subject of slavery: a muscular, solemn-faced boy named John, who was to go through fire and bloodshed and hatred to a high gallows and step off into strange legend.

At first things went well. Jesse Grant saved his money, and presently he went into a business partnership in the town of Ravenna. Then he was knocked back on his heels by the perennial scourge of the Ohio frontier, a malady known to settlers as "fever and ague" and to more modern medicine as malaria. (A Cleveland newspaper at about that time announced a sovereign remedy: "It is simply common salt. A teaspoonful taken in water, and a teaspoonful deposited inside each stocking next the foot, just as the chill is coming on. That is all there is of it.")

Frontier malaria was no joke. It put Jesse Grant out of action for a solid year. His money vanished, the partnership dissolved, he ran into debt, and when he was finally able to work he went down-state to Point Pleasant to ply his trade for a storekeeper who wanted to open a side-line business in leather goods. Jesse worked hard, paid off his debts — and, in the spring of 1821, married Hannah Simpson, daughter of a prosperous farmer.

It is possible to see more of Ulysses in Hannah Grant than in Jesse. She was quiet, self-contained, reserved; if her emotions ran strongly she made them run out of sight somewhere, so that the surface was never ruffled. Indeed, she carried this self-possession to the verge of outright eccentricity. When a horrified neighbor ran into the house to tell her that three-year-old Ulysses had taken a horse by the tail and was happily swinging there, in imminent danger of being kicked into the next county, she remarked that he would be all right — he "had a way" with horses. After this son grew world-famous she would quietly get up and leave the room if anyone praised him in her presence. She was to live beyond ninety, and to the end of her days was unshaken in the conviction that the nation was ruined beyond hope of recovery when the Democrats lost control of the government in 1860.

Ulysses was her firstborn, and if she had had her way he would have come down to history as Albert Gallatin Grant. (Albert Gallatin was a Pennsylvanian and so were the Simpsons, and the family greatly admired him). She was overruled. Her father thought Hiram a very handsome name, and her mother, who had been reading stories of the ancients, voted for Ulysses. Jesse sided with the old folks, and Hiram Ulysses it was.

A year after Ulysses was born, Jesse had regained his lost independence. With his debts paid and money laid by he moved to the county seat town of Georgetown, two dozen miles east — a pleasant place with a drowsy Southern-style public square surrounding a little courthouse, a town no bigger than Point Pleasant but more likely to grow. There Jesse bought land, built a house and opened his own tannery, and although he was never very popular with his fellow citizens — he was too boastful and contentious, and anyway he was a lone Yankee in an unmistakably Southern town — he quickly won a solid business success. His tanyard was a busy place. His teams plodded the country roads for miles, hauling hides and tanbark; to keep them busy, Jesse engaged also in general hauling, and eventually opened a livery stable. The Grants' brick home was enlarged, and self-educated Jesse proudly bought books for his library. He was comfortably well off while still comparatively young, and it was clear that he would be tolerably wealthy before he grew old.

Ulysses Grant, accordingly, had neither poverty nor deprivation in his youthful background. He was born into a home more prosperous than most, eldest son in a house where family affection was strong. The life about him was both exciting and leisurely — tense and aquiver with growth and vitality in an era of unimaginable development, but indolent and unhurried for all that . . . wagons creaking slowly along sandy roads, farms and villages savoring the peace of rising shadows in an eternal summer afternoon, something of the broad land's serenity flavoring the lives that were lived so close to the land. It was a good time to be a small boy in a small town. One would suppose that the boyhood of Ulysses Grant must have been very happy.

Yet the story is that an unhappy childhood left a lifelong mark on him. He was shy and sensitive. His unpopular braggart father drew unpopularity on him, his own quaint boyhood blunders made him a laughingstock, and he never forgot it or quite got over it.

So says the legend. The famous anecdote of Ulysses buying a colt reveals the distortions in it.

The boy was eight, a neighbor had a colt for sale, and Ulysses wanted it. His father gave him twenty-five dollars and some good Yankee advice about the way to drive a bargain. Ulysses went to the neighbor and innocently blurted out the whole story: "Papa says I may offer you twenty dollars for the colt, but if you won't take that I am to offer tweny-two and a half, and if you won't take that, to give you twenty-five." The story got around, everybody laughed, and Ulysses was reminded of it for years to come.

Yet the result was not a sensitive child driven in on himself, forced in self-defense to cultivate an impassive stolidity to protect a bruised ego and a crippled, tormented psyche. Note, to begin with, that Ulysses told the whole story on himself, when he finally wrote his memoirs: told it, moreover, not with the bitter grin of a man unveiling something that has hurt him all his life, but simply as a rather funny little story. (Note also that he had what he is not always given credit for, a dry but very perceptive sense of humor.) Note, finally, that the first chapter of his memoirs, in which he tells about his boyhood, has a little glow in it, as writing does when a man looks back on something pleasant. If those were dark years when lasting wounds were received, there is little hint of it in his reminiscences.

On the contrary, every recollection is of a singularly happy boyhood. As Hannah Grant said, Ulysses had a way with horses. Before he was in his teens he far outclassed his playmates in a field which, in that premechanical age, would win prestige and inflate a juvenile ego as nothing else possibly could. He was not yet ten when he was working as a teamster in jobs where all the other workers were grown men. He was known all over the county as a youngster with a quite unaccountable knack for breaking and training spirited colts; farmers brought such animals to him, and it was common for admiring crowds to gather in the village square and watch him. When people came to Jesse Grant's livery stable to hire transportation to some other town, Ulysses was very often the driver who took them there and then brought the team back. When a circus came to town and the ringmaster exhibited a trick horse, and offered a prize to anyone who could ride it around the sawdust circle, Ulysses usually won.

The boy also had a good head for business. The one thing he did not like was to work in his father's tannery, where his job usually was to feed tanbark into the hopper of a macerating machine. Jesse noticed, with stolid Yankee admiration, that when Ulysses was summoned to this job he would often give some other youngster ten or fifteen cents to take his place while he took one of the Grant teams out and got a hauling job that would net him a dollar or more. It was recalled, too, that when the boy was hired to drive someone to Cincinnati, he would hunt up a fare for the return trip before he started back. His father sent him on a business mission to Louisville while he was still so small that it was necessary to equip him with a letter certifying that he had permission to travel — otherwise hotel and steamboat men would have been likely to flag him down as a runaway. One odd quirk was noticed: when the boy made a trip and accidentally drove past his destination, he would make any kind of roundabout circuit to get back to it, even at the cost of considerable trouble. He had some deep-seated reluctance to retrace his steps.

Schooling in small-town Ohio in the 1820's and 1830's was adequate, perhaps, but not fancy. The school usually had one room and one teacher, invariably a male. Corporal punishment was so universal that a whole bundle of birch switches might be worn out in a day, and it was so little objected to that the teacher had no trouble getting his pupils to fetch a new supply. Lessons were learned by rote. Ulysses remembered being taught so many times that A Noun Is the Name of a Thing that "I finally came to believe it." He got his share of the birchings, showed aptitude for arithmetic but no especial ability in anything else, and was brought to outright mutiny by one teacher who introduced a course in public speaking.

At fourteen he went to spend a year in an academy at Maysville, Kentucky, where lived other Grants. Jesse wanted his firstborn to get the best education available. But the academy seems to have offered just about what the school at Georgetown was offering, and Ulysses found himself once more called upon to observe that a noun is the name of a thing. If, in the end, this sort of schooling did enable him to pass the West Point entrance examinations, it was because the examinations then were tailored to fit nominees who came from exactly such schools.

West Point was strictly Jesse's idea. Back of the idea was the notion that the Military Academy offered a good education at no cost. (Jesse's Yankee thrift was sharpened, as Ulysses reached his mid-teens, by the panic of 1837.) His attitude was common. Many West Point graduates left the army after brief service and took good jobs in civilian life; if the nation was not yet really convinced that its small army needed trained officers or a special institution to provide their training, it had a high opinion of the instruction which the Military Academy offered. It turned out engineers, for one thing, and in the fast-growing, feverishly building new country, engineers were in great demand.

Jesse made the West Point plan alone. Ulysses had made

it clear that he would have nothing to do with the tannery, once he was grown, but beyond that he had nothing especial in mind. He rather thought it would be nice to be a farmer, or perhaps an Ohio River trader, but the notion of being a soldier never entered his head.

At the end of 1838, when Ulysses, currently a student in a Presbyterian academy in Ripley, Ohio, was home for the Christmas holidays, he saw his father open and read a letter from Senator Thomas Morris, one of Ohio's early antislavery leaders. Jesse looked up from the letter and remarked that it looked as if the appointment was coming through.

Appointment? What appointment?

Why, to West Point, of course.

Ulysses replied flatly that he would not go. Jesse said he thought he would. Years later, Ulysses recalled that "I thought so too, if he did." So that was settled, and the boy resigned himself.

His reluctance to go to West Point was simple: he did not think he was clever enough to complete the course, and he could not bear the idea of failing. Four other boys from Georgetown had gone to the Military Academy. Three had been graduated but the fourth had flunked out, and his family had felt so disgraced that they had forbidden him to come home. It was all too easy for Ulysses to imagine the same thing happening to him.

Actually, the appointment was not quite settled. Senator Morris did not have a vacancy to fill, and he advised Jesse to apply to Congressman Thomas L. Hamer. The trouble with that was that Hamer and Jesse had had a quarrel — both were Democrats, but as a businessman Jesse had criticized Andrew Jackson, and one word had led to another — and they were no longer on speaking terms. But Jesse was bound that his boy should go to West Point, and he swallowed his pride and wrote to Hamer. Hamer welcomed the chance to end the quarrel, and he hurriedly made out the appointment papers. In his haste he made a little slip that had far-reaching effects.

He got a little mixed on that Grant boy's name. He remembered that Jesse always called him Ulysses, and he remembered that Hannah Grant's maiden name was Simpson; and so the papers, as he filled them out, conferred a West Point nomination on Ulysses Simpson Grant, the name got into the War Department records that way — and, as the young man who had to wear the name found out, that was that.

Ulysses himself had always preferred the name Hiram, and signed himself that way throughout his boyhood; it was too easy for people to twist Ulysses into "Useless." But the laws of the Medes and the Persians were no more immutable than the records of the War Department, and there was nothing anybody could do about it. There it was, from now on — U. S. Grant, forever.

3. *Dreams of a Young Soldier*

NEVER AGAIN will anyone see what U. S. Grant saw when he went from the Ohio Valley to the Hudson in May, 1839.

The rickety old side-wheelers are long gone from the rivers, and in the Pennsylvania mountain valleys there are neither canals nor boats to float on them. The stagecoach no longer trundles along a dusty road, creaking and jangling and lurching with make-believe haste, and the archaic twelve-miles-an-hour railroad trains have evolved into something very different. There was a springtime light on the land then, a time to take a last look around before the beginning of unending change; and the young fellow who, in his own strange way, was to be the instrument and the symbol of much of that change came East to begin training for his job.

First there was the steamboat to Pittsburgh. The boat was on no regular schedule, but stopped whenever and wherever there was a passenger or a parcel of freight. It took three days to get to Pittsburgh, and that was all right with young Grant; he liked to travel, and anyway he rather dreaded getting to his destination. At Pittsburgh he chose to go to Harrisburg by canalboat rather than by stagecoach, simply because the boat would go more slowly. He went from Harrisburg to Philadelphia by railroad — the first he had ever seen, except for the contrivance that hauled canalboats over the Allegheny crossing — and he took his time to see the sights in Philadelphia and later in New York.

But he could not make the trip last forever. Finally he presented himself at the Military Academy, made a futile effort to persuade the authorities that his name really was Hiram Ulysses rather than Ulysses Simpson, passed the entrance examination without difficulty, and found himself a cadet.

His old fear of academic failure quickly vanished. Without overtaxing himself, he found, he could maintain a safe if not impressive passing grade. An instructor recalled later that although Grant had "an undoubted capacity to excel," he did not shine. In mathematics he was very good, but in all other subjects he was content to drift along in effortless mediocrity. He was at West Point solely because his father had sent him there; nothing about the place touched his ambition.

Indeed, he quickly acquired a positive distaste for military life. He detested drill and parades. (The fact that he was so tone-deaf that he could hardly keep step when his company marched to music probably had a little to do with this.) West Point smartness was not for him. Never could the army quite eradicate his faint air of slouchiness, or take the little stoop out of his shoulders, or induce him to pay much attention to the spit-and-polish aspect of soldiering. Quite frankly, he wanted nothing on earth so much as to get out of the place and return to Ohio.

Many men in Congress then wanted to abolish the academy. They considered it antidemocratic and saw perils in the creation of a cohesive officer corps. During Grant's plebe year a bill to do away with the academy was debated, and Cadet Grant hoped against hope that it would pass. When it failed he was gloomy — the one chance to make an honorable exit seemed to have gone.

A bit later his dissatisfaction grew so sharp that he actually invited expulsion. One Benny Havens ran a famous pub, a mile from the military reservation, strictly off limits, with dismissal threatened for any cadet who patronized it. Naturally, most of the cadets went there at one time or another, using all manner of dodges to go unseen. But Grant boldly donned his dress uniform one day, walked out the main gate and went to Benny Havens's ostentatiously. Authority saw his going and his return, says tradition — and simply took it for granted that someone must have authorized the trip. Grant was not even asked to explain.

He never again invited expulsion — and never forgot the little object lesson: that a man who is bold enough can sometimes get away with a great deal.

One thing fired his imagination and his ambition briefly, at the end of his plebe year. General Winfield Scott visited the academy and reviewed the cadets.

Scott had great fame and great ability, plus a strong taste for pomp and circumstance. He was one of America's genuinely great soldiers, and he looked the part. He even impressed U. S. Grant, which very few men were ever able to do. As the cadet corps paraded past, Grant had a wild moment of vision — someday, if all went well, he himself might wear a general's uniform and stand there taking the salute of the corps of cadets.

The vision passed, and Grant did not again imagine a great future for himself as a soldier. What he did imagine was much more prosaic. If he could finish his course and get a diploma, he might, with luck, be detailed as instructor in mathematics at the academy. After that, he believed, it would be easy to win "a permanent position as professor in some respectable college." But the decision to seek this goal did not make a better student of him. To the end he jogged along easily in the academic middle of his class.

On his classmates Grant made little impression, except for one thing: he was far and away the best horseman in the academy, surpassing even the Southerners, who behaved as if they had been born to the saddle. The prestige of taking a horse over a higher jump than anyone at West Point was all Grant's, and the memory of it stuck. James

Longstreet, who was with him in the academy for three years, confessed long afterward that he could remember almost nothing about him except that Ulysses had a way with horses.

There was, of course, the nickname. By army decree he was now U. S. Grant, and the initials hit their obvious target. From his first day at the academy he was "Uncle Sam," or plain Sam Grant in casual daily usage. A few classmates remembered being struck by a quality of determination that seemed to lie somewhere under the surface, and after he became famous it was said that one classmate, upon graduation, had confided that "if a great emergency arises in this country during our lifetime, Sam Grant will be the man to meet it." George Deshon, a brilliant cadet who presently was to quit the army for the priesthood, predicted that Grant someday would prove himself the strongest man in the class.

In general, however, Grant was simply one of the throng, a shy and slightly countrified youngster who did not seem to be going anywhere in particular. Most of the cadets would undoubtedly have agreed with one who remarked, a generation later, that "no one could possibly be more surprised than myself at Grant's amazing success."

The summer furlough at the end of the second year was a brief interlude. Grant went back to Ohio — Jesse had sold the Georgetown tannery and had moved to the town of Bethel, twelve miles away — and at the end of his life Grant remembered that furlough as the happiest time he ever had. Jesse had bought a young horse that had never been broken to harness, and this horse was Sam's to tame and to ride . . . with quiet shaded roads to follow, girls to call on, relatives to visit, a natty blue and white uniform to wear, a hazy dreamy summer to drift through without cares or responsibilities. He was going to make his modest and unassuming way in the world, and in the end he was going to come back here, to the open fields and the peaceful lanes and the company of old friends: so ran the dreams of U. S. Grant, with everything ahead of him. His mother noticed that West Point had straightened him up and squared his shoulders a bit.

The last two years at the academy passed more rapidly — although, as Grant confessed, they still seemed about five times as long as Ohio years — and finally, in June, 1843, came graduation. Grant was almost precisely in the middle of his class, ranking number twenty-one in a class of thirty-nine. Since a graduate's choice of service depended on his class standing, Grant's range was limited. The *corps d'élite,* engineers, was hopelessly out of his reach, and so was the more lowly artillery. He could choose only between infantry and cavalry, and he naturally chose the cavalry. Unfortunately, the army then contained but one cavalry regiment, and the roster of its officers had no vacancies. Grant had to go into the infantry, and as he idled away his postgraduation furlough back in Ohio, he had the post tailor make and send him the handsome uniform worn by a brevet second lieutenant of infantry.

This furlough was like the other one, a time of pure enjoyment, and Grant rather looked forward to that new uniform. It would be pleasant to impress his former schoolmates, to say nothing of the girls. The big day came, finally; he togged himself out in his new finery, got out his horse, and went for a ride, feeling only a little lower than General Winfield Scott himself.

It was the very last time U. S. Grant ever really tried to strut in a uniform. A small boy in the street jeered at him for a no-account tin soldier, and a livery stable tough mocked him by parading about, barefooted and unkempt, in soiled nankeens tricked up with ribbons to resemble Grant's outfit. People laughed, and Grant had had enough.

Years later, when he was a lieutenant general commanding all the armies of the United States, he liked to go about in a private's blouse with his three stars stitched to the shoulders.

4. *Old Rough-and-Ready*

He was a brevet second lieutenant in the 4th U.S. Infantry, with an income of $779 a year and a fair prospect of returning to West Point before too long as an assistant instructor of mathematics. He had written to the authorities about it and the deal appeared to be set, and in his spare time now he was boning up with the textbooks. After that, eventually, there could be resignation and a berth in "some respectable college." Meanwhile there was a year or two of army routine to endure.

It did not begin badly. He was assigned to Jefferson Barracks, near St. Louis, as good a spot as the army had to offer. Largest military post in the country, garrisoned by sixteen companies of infantry, it occupied a seventeen-hundred-acre reservation, with quarters for officers and men lining three sides of a parade ground, and with plenty of space for gardens and lawns and trees. Commanding officer was Colonel Stephen Watts Kearny, rated one of the best men in the army, and if he was a stickler for discipline, he believed in making life comfortable for his juniors. If an officer did his daily tasks and was present for drill and roll call, the rest of his time was his own.

It did not take Grant long to find a good way to use his spare time. In his final year at West Point he had roomed with young Fred Dent, and although Dent had been sent to a distant post, the Dent family lived only five miles from Jefferson Barracks. To his lasting good fortune and happiness, Grant rode over to get acquainted.

The Dent place was known as White Haven. Farther north, it would have been called a farm and its owner a farmer. In the Missouri of the 1840's it was a plantation and Mr. Dent was a planter, and it was a conscious and not unsuccessful copy of the already legendary plantation of what even in its heyday seemed the Old South: pillared mansion, whitewashed slave quarters, colored children tumbling about the yard, plenty of good food to eat and plenty of good horses to ride, Old Marster sitting on his porch, afternoons, to look out over his acres, smoke a contemplative pipe, and if occasion afford to expound the doctrine of old-fashioned Democracy, with denunciation for all Whigs and outright fulmination against that developing species, the Yankee abolitionist. He was Colonel Dent, because he lived in a society where "Colonel" implied a certain social and economic standing. Like all proper members of that society he was hospitable, and young army officers from Jefferson Barracks were always welcome—especially one who had been young Fred's roommate.

What the Dent family saw when Grant came to call stayed to dinner, came again and then became the stead iest of visitors, was not at all the bearded and mature general officer known to a later generation. Grant was slender, then, even slight — he had suffered from "fever and ague" in his childhood, and for a time there was fear that he might be threatened by tuberculosis — and he was clean-shaven, with an uncommonly fair skin and delicate coloring, with silky, wavy hair and clear blue eyes. One of the Dent children remembered, long afterward, how the first time she saw him she told herself that he was "pretty as a doll." Colonel Dent tended to be somewhat opinionated and irascible — what Southern planter could be otherwise? — but he liked him well enough; Grant could sit on the veranda and talk politics without stirring up the least discord. Mrs. Dent was captivated from the start, and she used to say — often enough for the rest of the family to remember it later — that that young man was sure to make his mark in the world someday.

The important member of the family, however, was Julia, the Dents' seventeen-year-old daughter. She was at a boarding school in St. Louis when Grant first came to call, but after a few months she returned to White Haven. She was pretty, delicately rounded, graceful, with color and complexion to match Grant's, a talented horsewoman; in St. Louis she had been quite sought after, and in a modest way she had been what in those days they called A Belle. The young lieutenant began to go riding with her, and somehow he was appearing at the Dent plantation more and more often, staying for the evening meal — and, as he himself confessed afterward, enjoying himself a good deal more. He and Julia rode together, went on picnics and fishing trips, often enough in company with one or another of the younger children, sometimes with another officer

from Jefferson Barracks. (Longstreet was one who now
and then went to White Haven with Grant.) All in all,
month after leisurely month went by and life was very
pleasant, and four decades later Grant admitted that if
the 4th Infantry had just remained in St. Louis, "this life
might have continued for some years without my finding
out that there was anything serious the matter with me."

But the 4th Infantry was not going to stay in St. Louis,
and the dreamy, planless way of life in which nobody had
to think about tomorrow was going to end — for Lieutenant Grant and for everybody else in the country. It
would be hard to understand. The young lieutenant would
feel that evil and designing men were responsible and he
would blame them bitterly, and other Americans would
feel the same way, blaming different persons; and the
golden age was ending, the idyl was about over, and Sam
Grant's West Point training would not lead finally to the
muted respectability of some college campus.

For the United States was about to annex Texas.

Texas had been a province of Mexico, empty and un-
used and strangely silent. From the early 1820's, immi-
grants from the United States had colonized it, and in
1836 Texas had declared its independence and — in the
eyes of everyone but the government of Mexico — had
made that independence good. In the early 1840's, to nobody's surprise, Texas was about to become a state in the
American Union. Beyond Texas, immense and vibrant
with mystery and promise, lay a prize whose full value
could not yet even be guessed: the rest of the great American land mass. California and the Southwest, the Pacific
coast with its infinite beaches breaking the surf of a ground
swell that came clear from the fabled Orient. The United

States was going to annex Texas and it was going to take this other prize as well, and although many people thought this very wrong, they could do nothing to prevent it. And when all of the surface reasons for annexation are added up, there remains what was perhaps the most important of all, an old fundamental element in the American consciousness: the feeling that destiny somehow faces west.

As a preliminary step, the government in the spring of 1844 sent the 4th Infantry down into Louisiana, to camp on a sandy pine ridge overlooking the Red River Valley not far from the town of Natchitoches. Ostensibly the regiment was there to prevent filibustering into Texas, but everybody knew better. All his life, Grant retained the belief which he then formed — that the war which was about to come of it all was "one of the most unjust ever waged by a stronger nation against a weaker."

As it happened, Grant had gone to Ohio on leave just before the regiment got its marching orders. A fellow officer wrote and told him what had happened, and the knowledge that he would no longer be stationed in St. Louis led Grant to see his delightful friendship with Julia Dent in an entirely new light. Returning from leave, he went out to White Haven before following his regiment to Louisiana, and when he came back he and Julia were engaged.

The tour of duty in Louisiana was more like active service than garrison duty in St. Louis had been. Camp life was enjoyable and the air was good — the place was known as "Camp Salubrity" — and Grant was out in the open from dawn to dusk, most of the time on horseback. He stopped boning up on mathematics; there was no time for it now, and anyway it was clear that no young infantry of-

ficer was going to go back to the academy to teach until
this fuss with Mexico was settled.

Doing all of this, Grant regained his health. He grew
heavier and solider, and he lost the ominous little cough
which he had had so many years. Later on he was to con-
clude that the government gave him back his strength and
indeed saved his life by making him get ready to fight
in a war of which he thoroughly disapproved.

Among the older officers the approach of war had the effect of separating the sheep from the goats.

Since there was no retirement system, an officer who got
past middle life — and hence was unemployable in the civilian world — would hang on to his commission up to the
actual moment of physical dissolution, since to leave the
army would be to starve. The list was cluttered with aging
colonels and lieutenant colonels who were of no earthly
use but of whom the army had no decent way to rid itself.
As war drew near, many of these old crocks discovered
that they had physical infirmities which would confine
them to garrison duty and prevent them from serving in
the field. Yet there were pathetic exceptions, here and
there. The 4th Infantry was commanded by an aged Colonel Vose, who had not stepped on the drill field for years.
The old colonel did not intend to miss any fighting, however, and he unexpectedly came to Camp Salubrity and
creaked out to the parade ground to put his regiment
through its drill. After a few minutes of the unaccustomed
exertion, he dropped dead.

On March 1, 1845, the bill annexing Texas to the
United States became law, and the officers at Camp Salubrity correctly assumed that they would soon be moved
much closer to the Rio Grande. War was certain now, and

they made their last preparations in different ways. Grant made his way by getting a furlough and hurrying north to White Haven, where he formally asked Colonel Dent for Julia's hand.

Colonel Dent's enthusiasm was not overwhelming. Army pay was notoriously low and promotion was even more notoriously slow, and a very junior second lieutenant was not a good matrimonial prospect. But Colonel Dent ran into what many another parent has run into in similar case: his wife and daughter made common cause against him, and his consent presently was forthcoming. When Grant rejoined the regiment the betrothal was formal. Marriage, of course, would have to wait until the war was over.

The regiment moved, first to New Orleans and then down to Corpus Christi, in Texas. There the government was assembling what it called "the army of occupation": seven companies of cavalry, four of light artillery, and six regiments of infantry — regulars to a man, perhaps three thousand of them in all. In command was a soldier who was to put a lasting imprint on Grant's developing personality — Colonel Zachary Taylor, brigadier general by brevet, "Old Rough-and-Ready" by nickname.

Taylor was a natural. A professional soldier but not a West Pointer, he had fought in the War of 1812 and subsequently in many a campaign against the Indians. He had an ostentatious and wholly sincere dislike for military formality. By custom, he wore blue jeans, a long linen duster and a floppy straw hat, and he would lounge around headquarters like a seedy backwoods farmer. On the parade ground, when he sat his horse to review troops or to watch drill or maneuvers, he was as likely as not to sit sidesaddle, chewing tobacco and behaving like a man who casually watches the field hands harvest a crop. With Colonel Dent he shared the belief that a young army officer is not promising marriage material; ten years earlier he had refused to let his daughter marry young Lieutenant Jefferson Davis. (Not being the man to take no for an answer, Davis eloped with her in spite of the general.)

Zachary Taylor was the precise opposite of Winfield Scott, the first soldier to make a real impression on U. S. Grant. They had just one thing in common: both were first-rate fighting men. In Taylor's case, his reputation was such that his mere arrival at Corpus Christi made every officer assume that action would begin shortly. There could be no other reason to lead the government to put Zachary Taylor in charge of anything!

Scott had first showed Grant what the soldier incarnate might look like; now Taylor showed him the exact opposite. He might have been created expressly for the young officer who had been derided by village roughnecks for wearing a new uniform and who had thereby picked up a strong distaste for military display. He gave Grant one of the first lessons in the military art — that under all of the glitter and the drill and the show, the result on the field of battle was about all that really mattered. Back of the famous soldier who was to go slouching off to the supreme moment of his career at Appomattox Courthouse wearing a private's blouse, mud-stained pants and boots and no sword at all, stood somewhere the remembered example of Old Rough-and-Ready, who would have done it just the same way.

5. *Lessons in War*

I‌T WAS HARD to get the war started. The Mexican government refused to admit that Texas had ever won enough independence to enter the American union, but when the annexation was announced no Mexican army marched. There were angry threats and proclamations of defiance, but nothing actually happened. Zachary Taylor and his army of occupation camped unmolested at Corpus Christi, where the Nueces River came down to the Gulf.

It was important that they be molested. There was some doubt whether the American Congress would declare war otherwise, and the administration needed a war because it wanted Mexican territory which it could never get without fighting for it. As Grant saw it, Washington had to be able to show that American troops had been attacked and that war had begun by act of the Mexicans.

The Nueces River was supposed in a hazy sort of way to be the boundary between Mexico and Texas, but when three thousand American regulars had camped there for several months without trouble the authorities recalled that according to one old theory the ancient Mexican province of Texas had run all the way to the Rio Grande, one hundred and fifty miles farther on. The army of occupation, therefore, had better get on down to the Rio Grande, where Mexico was known to have an army. It seemed certain that this move would provoke the indispensable attack.

The move could not be made at once. Corpus Christi was hardly more than a frontier trading post set down in almost totally uninhabited territory. When Grant accom-

panied a troop train and cavalry escort back to San Antonio, one hundred and fifty miles by the roads as they
were then laid out, he saw no houses until within thirty
miles of San Antonio. A little later the army was to learn
that there was not a single human habitation between the
Nueces and the mouth of the Rio Grande. Before the advance could be made, supply dumps must be accumulated.
In the end the army stayed at Corpus Christi until March,
1846.

The stay was not unenjoyable. The men could swim and
fish in the Gulf, and there were immense quantities of
game to be shot by anyone who cared to tramp a few miles
inland. Grant went hunting once, with another officer, but
the sport was not for him. Getting in among a prodigious
flock of wild turkeys, he became so interested just watching
the birds that he forgot to shoot any of them, and besides
he did not like to eat fowl of any kind. (He once explained, half apologetically, that "I never could eat anything that goes on two legs.")

If he did not care for hunting, he was able to indulge his
fondness for wild horses. Beyond the Nueces there were
herds of wild mustangs as extensive as the fabulous buffalo herds. Horses taken from these bands could be bought
for ridiculously low prices. Grant got a string and was very
well mounted for a second lieutenant of infantry who did
not, by army regulations, rate a horse at all. When three of
his horses ran away, officers remarked that "Grant has
lost five or six dollars' worth of horses." This, said Grant,
was a slander; the animals had been broken to the saddle when he got them, and the trio had cost nearly twenty
dollars.

Finally the great day came. Sick men and convalescents

were sent away by boat, adequate guards were left to look after public property, and the twenty-five hundred men who were to make the advance got under way, cavalry in the lead, three infantry brigades following at one-day intervals. After the Civil War, in which armies many times the size of this one moved on the same day over narrow roads through dense forests and across large rivers, Grant looked back with an amused chuckle at this elaborate care in moving three tiny brigades. But the U. S. Army at that time was mostly an aggregation of detachments used separately for fighting Indians or garrisoning sleepy forts. When actual war came the officers had to learn their trade, from Old Rough-and-Ready on down.

Reaching the mouth of the Rio Grande, Taylor built a fort on the northern side, left a small garrison in it, and pulled the rest of his men back to the principal advanced base of supplies, Point Isabel, twenty-five miles to the north, where food and munitions and reinforcements could be unloaded from ships. And on a morning early in May, the men at Point Isabel heard a distant fluttering rumble on the air and correctly identified it as the sound of gunfire. The Mexicans had risen to the bait at last and had attacked Taylor's little fort. The war was on.

Grant confessed that he did not like the sound. He disapproved of this war on principle, and in addition he could not find within himself that hot desire to get into combat which some officers professed to have. (Most of these, he commented, cooled off remarkably once the fighting started. Still, a few made their boasts good when the time came. It appeared that a braggart could be a brave man, after all.)

He did not have much time to analyze his emotions, fo

Taylor took his army to the scene of action as fast as he could, and on May 8, 1846, by a pretty stand of trees known locally as Palo Alto, half a dozen miles away from the beleaguered fort, the Americans encountered a Mexican army drawn up in battle array.

The Mexicans had much cavalry, which made a brave showing; the troops wore fancy uniforms of light blue and they carried lances, and the morning sunlight glinted and sparkled from the lance heads all along the line. Taylor got his troops into line of battle, and Grant looked at the twenty-five-hundred-man host and reflected that a general commanding so many men must carry an almost unbearable load of personal responsibility when he takes them into action.

Taylor did not seem worried. He brought his artillery up to the front, at intervals in the line of infantry — some brass six-pounders, a few twelve-pound howitzers, and a couple of long-range eighteen-pounders — and when all was ready he slouched around sidesaddle, his straw sombrero tilted back on his head, and ordered each company to send a detail back to a little stream to fill canteens for all hands. After every soldier had had his drink of fresh water the battle line began to roll forward, and a number of young officers who were to have important commands in an infinitely greater war fifteen years later got their first experience of battle.

It was a strange battle, fought mostly beyond infantry range. Infantry muskets then were smoothbores, chiefly flintlocks, and their range was very short; as Grant recalled, from a few hundred yards "a man might fire at you all day without your finding it out." All over the plain grew heavy grass, tall as a man's shoulder. When the Mexican artillery opened fire the ricocheting cannon balls cut odd wavy lanes through this grass, and American soldiers could see and dodge. (Some of them could dodge. Grant saw one cannon ball take off the head of an enlisted man in his regiment, break off the lower jaw of a captain, and drive the sickening fragments about in such a way as to knock down two or three other men.) Once the grass between the armies took fire, sending up blinding smoke, and the fighting stopped until this died down. Mexican cavalry tried to swing around and attack the American flank, and Taylor's artillery broke it up and sent it flying. The American artillery outranged the Mexican, and it was firing shell while the Mexicans fired solid shot. In the end it ruled the field and drove the Mexicans off in retreat. American losses had been unimportant — nine killed and fewer than fifty wounded.

The Mexicans did not retreat far. Next day the Americans found them drawn up in a good defensive position behind a little chain of ponds, with dense underbrush in front — a spot known as Resaca de la Palma. Here the conditions for artillery fire were not as good, and the infantry went forward into close action. During the temporary absence of his captain, Grant proudly took command of his company, got it forward through the chaparral, had the men lie down once when Mexican fire became very heavy, and at last burst out into the open and captured a Mexican colonel and a few privates. His elation dwindled when he learned that another detachment had been ahead of him and that his prisoners had already been captured. He reflected, also, that when he had his men lie down to save their lives they had already begun to do it without orders. In the end, he felt that "the battle of Resaca de la Palma would have been won, just as it was, if I had not been there."

It was indubitably a victory, no matter how little a junior infantry lieutenant had had to do with it. Taylor pushed on and relieved the fort at the mouth of the Rio Grande, and then crossed to the south bank of the river. He now commanded an army of invasion, not of occupation. The government began to send reinforcements — volunteer troops, mostly, men enlisted for one year, wild as so many unbroken mustangs, rowdy and insubordinate, but, as the event was to prove, good fighting men once they got into action.

Regular army officers wrung their hands because of the volunteers' lack of discipline, and accused them of indiscriminate rape and pillage among the Mexican population. It is noteworthy that Grant never joined in these complaints. He felt that all things considered the men behaved themselves pretty well; indeed, he remarked that because the army offered such a good cash market for their produce the Mexican people in the occupied zone were actually better off than ever before. More and more, Grant was taking Taylor's view of things: military formalities counted for little, all that mattered was what happened on the battlefield. Once he confessed that perhaps Taylor carried informality just a bit too far — usually there was nothing whatever about his costume even to show that he was connected with the army, let alone to indicate that he was in command!

The Mexicans withdrew beyond the Sierra Madre Mountains, and in midsummer, his army recruited to a strength of perhaps six thousand men, Taylor went after them. The Mexicans held Monterrey, which commanded a pass through the mountains. To reach them Taylor had to move one hundred miles up the Rio Grande and then make a hard, one-hundred-and-fifty-mile march overland. The move began late in August, and when it did Grant's military education took another long step forward. He was detailed as regimental quartermaster and commissary, responsible for the food, clothing, forage and equipment that had to be moved forward if the regiment was to exist; responsible also for organizing, loading and directing the inadequate wagon train and string of pack mules which carried it all.

It was inglorious drudgery, and Grant asked to be relieved and given a combat assignment. His application was rejected, and he glumly buckled down to a job for which in point of fact he was very well fitted. What he had to do now was not altogether unlike the work he used to do for his father back in Ohio. Grant knew how to handle animals, he had business ability and he showed a flair for the executive, managerial function — and, in sum, he filled his new role to the eminent satisfaction of everyone but himself. A future army commander could have had no more useful experience. Years later, people noticed that although an army commanded by Grant might be informal in its discipline and given to straggling and excessive foraging, its food and ammunition trains were always expertly handled and it was never held up by any failure in the movement of supplies and equipment.

The army got to Monterrey and found the Mexicans well dug in behind strong barricades, prepared to make a fight of it. Taylor looked the ground over carefully — one of his engineer officers was a testy lieutenant named George Gordon Meade, who classed volunteer troops with the Biblical plagues of locusts — and a furious two-day battle developed.

Grant managed to get into this fight. His story was that he went forward, after parking his trains, to see what his old regiment was doing. It was just beginning to make an assault, and "lacking the moral courage to return to camp," as his orders required, Grant went along with it. In any case the regiment got into a very hot spot, and before the battle ended Grant had distinguished himself by riding back through the embattled town to get ammunition and to take a message to division headquarters.

In the end the Mexican lines were broken and General Ampudia, the Mexican commander, offered surrender. Again Taylor gave Grant something to remember. He offered very liberal terms, letting the beaten army march away with flying colors, the infantry carrying its muskets, the artillery removing six fieldpieces. Ampudia withdrew seventy miles and an armistice followed. Taylor felt that the United States had shown that it could win the war about as it chose, and that the Mexican government might be ready to concede the point. The fighting stopped for a time, Taylor's army stayed in Monterrey, and there was fraternization between soldiers and civilians. Grant believed that because of Taylor's humane policy the Mexican civilians were eventually as sorry to see the American troops leave as they had been to see them arrive. Taylor had showed him something about the uses of magnanimity.

6. *Belfry at San Cosme*

THE WAR was going to be won. But it might not be won in the way the Administration wished. President James K. Polk was hard, smart and narrow, and if he was determined to ease the path of manifest destiny by adding part of Mexico to the United States he wanted the Democratic party to get the credit for it.

Winfield Scott was the country's top soldier, and he had a good war plan: land an army at Vera Cruz and march to Mexico City along the old route of Cortez. But Scott was a Whig and he was ambitious, and if he became conqueror of Mexico he might become President of the United States as well. Taylor was a Whig, too, but he was less ambitious; if there had to be a military hero from the opposition party, it was much safer to elevate Taylor than Scott. When the war began Scott was shelved and Taylor got the big job.

With Scott on the shelf, Taylor immediately became a national hero of such prominence that Taylor-for-President fires began to break out all over the country. It was necessary to deflate him, and that could be done only by resurrecting General Scott. Perhaps if there were two war heroes, both Whigs, they would kill each other off politically.

Thus the grand strategy of the war was abruptly turned upside down. The Scott war plan was brought out, Scott in person along with it, the push down across the Rio Grande was de-emphasized, and practically all of Taylor's regulars were taken away from him, put on transports, and sent down the Gulf to a rendezvous in the harbor of Antón

Lizardo, sixteen miles below Vera Cruz, where Scott's army was taking shape and accumulating supplies. (Left alone with an army of volunteers, Taylor refused to accept deflation, winning the battle of Buena Vista in a way that completely captivated the voters and made him an odds-on choice for the Presidency in 1848.)

Scott and Taylor were opposites, and unconsciously each man served as model for a talented junior; when the nation came to its supreme crisis, half a generation later, these juniors faced each other as leaders of rival armies. If the influence of Zachary Taylor is visible in the Civil War career of U. S. Grant, Winfield Scott's influence is equally visible in the Civil War career of Robert E. Lee.

The business of living and looking the part of a great soldier, with splendor worn as a familiar cloak about starred shoulders; the battle technique of bringing troops to the scene of action and then relying on subordinates to run things; the readiness to rely on sheer audacity in the face of an enemy of superior numbers — all of these, characteristic of Lee in Virginia, were equally characteristic of Scott in Mexico. Lee came to Vera Cruz as an engineer captain on Scott's staff. He never forgot what Scott taught him.

The administration gave Scott an army of between ten and twelve thousand men, and he made short work of Vera Cruz, landing beyond range of the city's guns, stringing entrenchments completely around the place, and then hammering it with siege guns until it surrendered. Like Taylor, Scott was magnanimous. Great pains were taken to conciliate the civilian population, and as a rigid disciplinarian Scott put a tighter rein on his volunteer troops than Taylor had ever attempted.

From the moment the city fell Scott was looking inland. Mexico City was two hundred and sixty miles away, by roads which led through formidable mountain passes. Scott's army was small, and he could see that it was not going to get any larger; Polk would send reinforcements, but these would do no more than balance losses due to battle and disease. As Scott considered the situation — early in April, 1847, just a year after Taylor struck the first blows up by the Rio Grande — it was obvious that he must move inland very soon. Yellow fever would strike the coastal region before long, and the unacclimated Americans must get out of the danger area and into higher altitudes.

Leaving behind only the sick, convalescents and a garrison for the captured forts, Scott started out for Mexico City in the middle of April, with perhaps ten thousand effectives. Fifty miles out he ran into the Mexicans at Cerro Gordo, a mountain pass where winding roads and breath-taking precipices made a frontal assault impossible. Scott sent his engineer officers out to find a feasible avenue of attack.

He was singularly blessed in his engineer officers. Besides Lee, there were gifted young lieutenants such as P. G. T. Beauregard, George B. McClellan, Isaac Stevens and G. W. Smith. These presently found a way to get men and guns far around on the Mexican flank and rear, across what had been thought to be wholly impassable ridges and gorges. Scott made the attack and drove the Mexicans in headlong route, capturing three thousand prisoners and much booty. The way to the interior was open.

Scott lost no time, and hurried on. There was a brief halt at Perote, an abandoned Mexican fortress, where volunteer regiments whose time was expiring were sent back to Vera Cruz. Then the army went on, following the famous road of Cortez, surrounded by constant rumors of attack but meeting no actual enemies. By mid-May the leading division occupied the important town of Puebla, better than halfway from Vera Cruz to the capital.

There was an interlude here while Scott waited for reinforcements. Grant was with the advance guard, still acting as quartermaster and commissary, and with wagons and pack trains he made many side trips to collect food and forage, with a small escort for protection against attack by the aimless, roving bands of Mexican cavalry. The country was surpassingly lovely and Grant was enjoying life; something about this land made a profound appeal to him, as it did to other American officers. The semitropical lushness of the landscape, the beauty of the mountains, the richness of the flowers and blossoms, which Cortez's own hard-boiled men-at-arms had noticed, made an unforgettable impression — these, and even more, the dreamy indolence of Mexican life, something that seemed to hang in the very air, as if people had infinite time at their disposal and so could afford to drift and idle and drowse. When Grant wrote about it, in his old age, it was like looking back on that sun-drenched Ohio boyhood, and he seemed to be writing an idyl.

It appealed to something basic, in him and in others. Limitless drive and energy lie in the American character, yet hand in hand with these go a talent for laziness, an ability to tilt the hatbrim down over the eyes and let things slide — queer dualism, native not only to U. S. Grant but to many others. (Native also, surprisingly enough, to a rawboned, all-thumbs young lieutenant of artillery in this expeditionary force who was to become famous later as Stonewall Jackson, an uncompromising Ironsides who was secretly bewitched by Mexico all of his life.) Heritage of the fever-and-ague of frontier days, perhaps? Or of the hot noonday of American sunlight, offering leisure in the shade at the edge of the harvest fields? Whatever it means, there it is, ineradicable: a trait, just incidentally, of the trained and conditioned athlete.

Several months passed. New troops came down from the north. Polk apparently failed to realize how many men were kept out of the ranks by illness (Scott had eighteen hundred men in an improvised hospital at Puebla), and Scott's strength was overestimated in Washington. When it came time to advance, Scott had to move with fewer than eleven thousand men. He perfected the organization of his army, Grant and his fellows collected foodstuffs, native Pueblans were hired to make shoes and clothing, and Polk's diplomats tried in vain to get the Mexican dictator, Santa Anna, to admit defeat and accept a peace. By August 6, 1847, it was plain that Santa Anna would not quit until an American army had captured his capital. All of the reinforcements that were going to come were on hand, and the army set out on the last leg of its long hike to Mexico City.

At this point Grant got one more lesson in strategy. By all of the textbooks, an invading army must retain firm contact with its base of supplies. Yet for Scott this was impossible, unless he used most of his army to protect the supply line. Boldly and simply, therefore, he cut loose from his base altogether. The army could collect food as it moved, and there would be time enough to reopen a line of supply after the enemy had been whipped. (Cortez had set the pattern, centuries earlier, when he burned his ships on the Vera Cruz beach, giving his troops the simple imperative: Conquer or die!) As a supply officer, Grant now learned what all of this meant and how it was done, and the lesson stuck.

The march to the valley of Mexico was unopposed. Grant wondered why the Mexicans failed to make a stand in the lofty pass over Rio Frio Mountain, eleven thousand feet above the sea. From the high mountains the soldiers looked down on the broad valley, with its sparkling lakes, its imposing capital, its towns and villages and its green fields, and they marveled as Cortez's soldiers had done; then they went down into the valley for the final act of the drama, and by August 18 they were in camp just eleven miles south of the central plaza of Mexico City.

The last act turned out to be long, and if the going so far had been easy it suddenly became very rough. Young Captain Lee again distinguished himself, finding a route for an army column across what was supposed to be a pathless waste of splintered lava. Scott credited him with "the greatest feat of physical and moral courage" of the entire campaign, and Lee's reconnaissance led to victory. American troops came in on the flank of a Mexican line at Contreras, and Santa Anna's outer chain of defense was cracked. When he wrote his report on the battle, Scott unblushingly remarked that he did not believe there was a more brilliant and decisive victory on record, and Grant noted that the general could sing his own praises without the least embarrassment. Next day there was a hard, grinding fight along the Churubusco Canal that drove the Mexicans back into their inner lines. It was hoped that Santa Anna would be ready to admit defeat now, so Scott negotiated an armistice, put his army into camp, and let Polk's envoys resume their peace talks with the Mexicans.

Nothing came of this. Santa Anna had no intention of giving up, and when Scott found that the Mexican was using the armistice simply to rebuild his army he canceled the truce and on September 7 he moved forward once more.

More hard fighting: a vicious struggle for a strong point built around a suburban mill, Molino del Rey, led to an even more desperate fight for famous Chapultepec, the "hill of the grasshoppers," where Montezuma had had a pleasure garden and where the Mexican Republic had a military college. Grant managed to get into this action, and in his memoirs he commented wryly that he had repeated his exploit of Resaca de la Palma — that is, he had gallantly captured a group of Mexicans who, as he later found out, had previously surrendered to somebody else.

When Chapultepec fell the Mexicans were driven back to the walls of Mexico City itself, with the Americans in hot pursuit. In the final storming of the last defenses Grant performed a military feat at which he did not have to look back with a tolerant smile. He led an artillery detachment in past an unguarded flank, got a light howitzer up into a church belfry, and laid a hot and effective fire on the Mexican defenders of a key bastion in the suburb of San Cosme. (His division commander saw it and sent an officer to find out who was doing all of this and to tell him to keep it up: a Lieutenant John C. Pemberton, whom Grant was to meet again at Vicksburg, Mississippi.)

Then the defenses cracked all along the line, American patrols burst in with bitter hand-to-hand, house-to-house fighting — and Santa Anna evacuated the city, and on September 14 the civil authorities came out to assure Scott that there would be no more resistance. The American army paraded in, the American flag went up over the presidential palace, and unvarnished democracy had followed the conquistadores to the halls of Montezuma.

An incalculable step toward the future had been taken. Because of this war, the United States now would go coast to coast, and in time it would look across the Pacific toward Asia, and the ripples from this homespun conquest would go on and on. New energies would be released and new powers would be built up, and in years to come Grant would believe that the Mexican War had made the Civil War inevitable. He would reflect that nations, like individuals, are punished for their sins.

There would be a state of war for months to come, while the negotiators haggled over the price of southwestern real estate and the United States Congress argued about a pestiferous little legislative rider known as the Wilmot Proviso. But to all intents and purposes the war was over. The army remained in the Mexican capital through fall and winter, and Grant continued to serve as quartermaster and comissary officer. In that job he showed business ability. Instead of drawing government-issue bread he drew the equivalent weight in flour, as the regulations said he might, and hired Mexican bakers to make bread of it. Since this produced much more bread than the regiment needed he sold the surplus for cash and turned the money over to the regimental fund. Proudly he noted that in two months he made more money for the regimental fund than his own pay amounted to for the entire war.

He was a first lieutenant now, promoted to fill a vacancy

created by an older officer's death in the last day's fighting. He also won a brevet captaincy, and he was mentioned in the official reports for the feat in the San Cosme belfry.

Yet if distinction and advancement were what he was after, his record was just average. All of the young regular officers had done well. Some, like handsome Captain Lee, would be marked men from now on. Most of Grant's war service had been in the unglamorous supply train, which brought nobody any headlines. Peace was coming, promotion would be slow, and the shock of war had broken the sketchy arrangements he had made about that instructorship at West Point. He would have to go back to garrison duty somewhere as a first lieutenant, in a career which he had never wanted to enter, and there did not seem to be any way by which he could soon get out of it.

But what he wanted chiefly was to get back to the United States to marry Julia Dent.

7. *Time of Seasoning*

MATERIAL SUCCESS has always seemed the goal, and the American people have won more of it, perhaps, than anyone else on earth. Yet their hearts have never really been in it, and they have not actually had much of a knack for it, and their record is full of ghost towns and lost men and pathetic little paths that go down to nowhere.

The truth is that the enormous drive and energy that won a continent and reshaped world history are always evoked by some undefined goal. The capacity for failure, therefore, is always present, because neither success nor failure in the ordinary meaning of the words is quite what the American really has on his mind.

So we have Ulysses Grant, who was no part of a mystic and who never suspected himself of wanting anything in particular beyond a chance to enjoy life doing congenial work — and who, somehow, was a great man whenever he served a cause and a flat failure whenever he tried to follow the main chance. The soldier who could manage an army as well as any man in American history could never manage his own affairs when those affairs were all he had to worry about.

The war with Mexico officially ended in the spring of 1848. The army came back to the United States, and as soon as he could arrange it Grant went to St. Louis and Julia Dent became his wife.

Grant was supremely fortunate in his marriage. There was in him a great loneliness hidden under a wistful shyness, a groping for understanding, a profound need for genuine communication with another human being. Fulfillment for all of this he found with his wife. The remark that is casually and inaccurately made about many men was literally true, with him: there never was any other woman in his life. So completely did she possess his spirit and his imagination that when she was not with him he seemed to be emotionally crippled. In later years, when some men worried (perhaps more than they really needed to) about whether he might stay on the right track, they knew there was always one remedy for any disturbed state he was in: get Mrs. Grant to him and he would be all right again.

For the next four years life was comparatively smooth

and uneventful; duty with the 4th Infantry at various Great Lakes posts, principally Detroit, with the round of professional and social activities which generations of young lieutenants and their wives have known at American army posts in peacetime. A son was born, named Frederick Dent Grant. The chance of a teaching appointment faded out and at last was forgotten. At thirty, Grant had settled into the groove, a career officer in a small army; he did not especially like it, but he had Julia and the baby, and it appeared that soon there would be another child — and, all in all, Lieutenant Grant was happy enough.

Then came change: the beginning of a period of bleak misery and incredible bad fortune and seemingly irretrievable failure.

In the spring of 1852 the War Department transferred the 4th Infantry to the Oregon country. Headquarters were to be at Vancouver Barracks, on the Columbia River, and the regiment's different companies would occupy a string of little forts in the Northwest. Since he was still regimental quartermaster, Grant would be at Vancouver.

It was an impossible trip for Julia, with two small children. Grant talked of resigning from the army. But he was thirty and it was late to begin a brand-new career, and at last it was arranged that Julia would stay with Jesse Grant in Ohio. Later it might be possible for her to take the children West and rejoin her husband. Meanwhile, Grant must go with his regiment.

The 4th Infantry contained seven hundred officers and men, in eight companies, and it moved by steamer from New York to Panama, across the Isthmus by dugout canoe and muleback, and on to San Francisco and Vancouver by steamer. The voyage was a nightmare. The steamers were grossly overcrowded, and at the Isthmus the contractor who was to provide transportation over to the Pacific side ran out on the job; at which moment, with the regiment struggling through tropical jungles, there came an attack of Asiatic cholera.

As quartermaster, responsible for transportation and for regimental property, Grant was busy enough. Somehow he got the well and the sick across the Isthmus, got hospital tents erected on the Pacific shore, scraped together means to carry baggage and supplies across, arranged for burial of the dead and found room on a steamer for all who had escaped the malady. Quarantine was enforced; it was six weeks before the regiment could sail, and it did not reach Vancouver until late in September.

At Fort Vancouver began bad times for Lieutenant Grant.

The California gold rush had inflated prices all up and down the Coast, and army officers would have starved if the government had not allowed them to buy their food from the commissary, at East-Coast wholesale prices. (Grant remarked that the pay of an army captain would not have hired a cook; the cook could do better on the outside.) Since the only thing Grant wanted was to bring his family West, he had to find some way to make extra money, and he tried a number of business ventures.

With several other officers he rented land along the river, bought horses, farm inplements and seed, and planted potatoes. Food prices in California were so high that this seemed a sure-fire way to make money. But the Columbia rose in flood and destroyed most of the crop — which was no great loss, after all, because everyone else on the West

Coast had planted potatoes too, and the price fell so low it did not pay to dig the crop.

Then it developed that ice was scarce in San Francisco. Grant and some others had one hundred tons of ice cut in the river, and sent it down by schooner; the schooner met head winds, took six weeks to make the trip, and arrived to find that shiploads of ice had just come in from Alaska and that the market was broken. This investment was a total loss.

Grant and a friend bought hogs from settlers and shipped them to San Francisco, only to run into another falling market and lose several hundred dollars. They bought chickens and chartered a schooner to take them down, and all of the chickens died en route. On a trip to San Francisco, Grant and other officers rented a vacant rooming house and hired an agent to operate it as a club and billiard room; accommodations were short, San Francisco was full of unattached males, and the idea looked sure-fire. But the agent decamped with the funds, and one more project had lost money instead of making money.

This was just the beginning.

Grant was promoted captain and transferred to command a company at Humboldt Bay, California. Now he was a line officer, not a quartermaster; his duties were routine and utterly boring, and his work no longer provided protection against the bitter homesickness which, other officers noticed, had beset him as soon as his ship left New York. Julia and the children were away off in Ohio, everything that he tried which promised to bring them to him failed, it might be years before he could see them . . . and Captain Grant took to drink.

Actually, he seems not to have taken to it as hard as the

tradition says he did. The army was a hard-drinking outfit in those days, especially in remote posts like Humboldt
Bay where officers did not have their families with them
and found their surroundings unbearably dull. Almost everybody drank, and drank quite a lot, and while it would
appear that Grant drank more than was good for him, nobody would ever have heard anything about it except for
two little handicaps. Grant was a man with whom a little
whiskey went a long way, so that every drink he took
showed on him, and he was serving under a cantankerous
officer who happened to dislike him personally.

Brevet Colonel Robert C. Buchanan was excessively
"old army," as soldiers of that day used the term, even for
the old army itself. He had been president of the officers'
mess at Jefferson Barracks when Grant was first stationed
there, and he and Grant had had a passage at arms about
some little thing — apparently nothing more serious than
Grant's way of being slightly tardy at meals. Whatever it
was, it had soured Buchanan on Grant and he had not forgotten about it.

It does not take much to make a man like Buchanan give
a junior officer the worst of it, since his type rides the
younger officers down anyway on general principles. Buchanan cracked down hard on Grant. Just what took place
is in some dispute, but the generally accepted story is that
he gave Grant the option of resigning or of standing trial
on formal charges of misconduct.

Grant could almost certainly have won if he had stood
trial. After all, the army in those days just did not cashier
officers for drinking unless a bender of earth-rocking pro-
portions had been involved. But to stand trial was un-
thinkable, because in such case the whole sorry story would

inevitably come to Julia's attention. Anyway, Grant had had all of the army he could take.

In the spring of 1854 Grant resigned, took ship for the East, reached New York broke, borrowed money from an officer friend named Simon B. Buckner in order to pay his hotel bill, repaid Buckner when a draft from Jesse reached him, and then went to Ohio to rejoin his family — a civilian for the first time since he had set out for West Point.

His troubles were not over.

Colonel Dent had given Julia sixty acres of unimproved land not far from St. Louis, and on this land Grant resolved to become a farmer. The land must first be cleared of timber, and Grant attended to this himself, making a modest income by hauling the wood to St. Louis in a wagon and peddling it to anyone who would buy. Now and again, on the streets, he would meet army officers he knew. They agreed that Sam Grant looked seedy — a little more stooped, a stubble of beard on his face, wearing a battered hat and a faded army overcoat — and a few perceptive ones, like Longstreet, could see that he was sensitive about poverty. Since the army was a tight little organization in which everybody knew everybody else, it was as gossipy as a ladies' bridge-luncheon club, and exaggerated tales about Grant's troubles on the West Coast had made the rounds. His appearance at St. Louis as, apparently, a down-and-out wood peddler seemed to confirm the worst that had been said. It might be noted, however, that officers who met him in St. Louis reported that he was not drinking now.

There were two years of backbreaking work. The land was cleared and prepared for planting. Grant squared logs and built a house, into which he and his little family moved, and although he was woefully short of capital it looked as if the worst might be over. But just as the first real crop was harvested the panic of '57 hit the country, farm prices dropped almost to zero, and the year's work went for nothing. The next year brought a different kind of bad luck: an unseasonable cold snap in June ruined the crop, and then the old enemy of Grant's childhood, fever and ague, struck him once more, and for six months he was a semi-invalid hardly able to move about the house.

Desperate, he sold the farm, taking a cottage in St. Louis in part payment. There he went into a partnership in a real estate office. The event quickly showed that whatever U. S. Grant might be fitted for, selling real estate and collecting rents did not belong on the list. The venture paid him less than his expenses. An attempt to get an appointment as county engineer fell through. Then the man who had bought his farm could not meet his payments, and that modest source of income dried up. At one time Grant wangled a little job in the St. Louis customhouse, but it was shot out from under him within weeks when a new customs collector took office and fired the entire staff.

Once, during these St. Louis days, Grant met another ex-officer whom he had known slightly at West Point, a man in nearly as bleak a fix as himself — William Tecumseh Sherman, who had left the army to become a banker, had failed, and now considered himself "a dead cock in a pit." Two former army officers, getting on into middle life, loaded with debts, stopping on the street to compare notes, agreeing that West Point offered poor training for nonmilitary pursuits. . . .

In 1860 Grant was driven to unconditional surrender. He had sworn, as a boy, that once he was grown he would do anything on earth except work in his father's tannery. Now he was thirty-eight, he had three children, debts, no income and no prospects; and he went to Jesse Grant and asked for a job.

Jesse gave him a job. (Jesse could have extended more of a helping hand than he did, and he could have extended it much earlier, but Grant left no hint of a complaint on the record.) Actually, it was better than Grant anticipated. He did not have to go to the tannery itself. Jesse had opened a leather store in the mining-boom town of Galena, Illinois, and his two younger sons were running it for him. In this store Ulysses was given a clerkship. The pay was moderate but there seems to have been some sort of profit-sharing arrangement, and any port looked like a good one in the storm that had been breaking over Grant's head. He moved his family to Galena, took a house there, and set out to be a businessman.

The worst of it all was over, although no soothsayer could have guessed how fantastically the road was going to spiral upward. Oddly enough, those hardscrabble years may not have been quite as somber to the man and woman who lived through them as they now seem to have been. Years later, when he was living in the White House, Grant met an old acquaintance from St. Louis, to whose house he used to deliver cord wood — wood which he himself had cut and hauled and which he piled on the buyer's fuel pile, going to the door afterward to get his money. He began to talk about the old days, and unexpectedly he remarked: "Those were happy days. I was doing the best I could to support my family."

Once during those hard days a seamstress was in the Grant home to help with some sewing. Mrs. Grant quietly remarked: "We will not always be in this condition." Her confidence in Grant never wavered, and Grant knew it, and toward the end of his life he told a friend: "I have seen some hard times in my life, but I never saw the moment when I was not sure that I would come out ahead in the end."

People who saw Grant during the last days in St. Louis remembered that he appeared sad and discouraged — and yet this, apparently, was less because of his own troubles than because he saw what other thoughtful men were see- ing then: the approaching disruption of the Federal Union. He had voted for James Buchanan, the Democrat, in 1856, fearing that a Republican victory would goad the South into secession. He had followed the Lincoln– Douglas debates attentively, considering himself a Douglas Democrat, and he wrote that when he heard Southern friends discussing a breakup of the Union as casually as if they were talking about a tariff bill, "it made my blood run cold."

Slowly his ideas were changing. He had lived in a slave state, he despised abolitionists, his wife owned slaves given her by her father, he himself had acquired ownership of a field hand from Colonel Dent. Yet in 1859, when he was giving up farming and was desperately pressed for money, and the one slave he owned could have been sold for a thousand dollars, he executed papers of manumission and gave the man his freedom.

Now he was living in Illinois, and the storm clouds were banked up black and ugly on the country's horizon. What- ever the bleak years had really meant to him, they had somehow seasoned him. He was ready to be used, now, and the time was at hand when the country was going to find a use for him.

The Great Commander

---

1. *Looking Down the River*

His EXCELLENCY, Governor Richard Yates, burly and capable and badly overworked, was slightly puzzled.

By ability, by training and by general background, this quiet Captain Grant was a natural for military command. He was all out for the Union, he had helped to arouse patriotic sentiment at Galena and had done his part with the recruiting and the drill, and he had been most useful as a clerk in the state adjutant general's office. Currently, he was temporary mustering officer at Camp Yates, where the state's raw levies were quartered. But somehow he did not seem to want to rise any higher.

With ten new volunteer regiments being raised, and with half the able-bodied adults in Illinois, seemingly, pulling wires to become majors or colonels, it was precisely the well-qualified Captain Grant who did not appear interested. Several regiments had offered to elect him colonel but he had refused to be a candidate. He remained a civilian, apparently content to be nobody much, always smoking a clay pipe, quietly and competently doing his job but displaying no ambition whatever. As an experienced politician Governor Yates could appraise the self-seekers. But what did you do with an odd fish like this?

Actually, the governor had misinterpreted things. Captain Grant did want a commission. His trouble was that he was congenitally and totally unable to push himself forward.

He had written to the War Department, citing his record and suggesting that he might be qualified to command a regiment. Nothing had come of it. (Years later his letter was found in a forgotten file. Apparently no one had ever read it.) He had tried to offer his services to an old army acquaintance named George B. McClellan, who was a glittering major general of volunteers in Ohio, but McClellan had been too busy to talk to him. A similar offer to an old West Point friend, Nathaniel Lyon, now commanding at St. Louis, had no better luck. U. S. Grant was stumped. His work at Springfield was nearly finished, and it began to look as if he would soon be back in the leather store.

About this time Governor Yates expressed his bewilderment in a conversation with a friend of Grant's. The friend set him straight. He pointed out that Captain Grant was a regular army man by training, and personally diffident to boot. In his book, officers were never "candidates" for anything, didn't get elected to anything, and never asked favors of politicians. If there was a job for this man to do the governor could just appoint him without asking him about it.

As it happened, Governor Yates did have a job to fill. A riotous volunteer outfit, tentatively known as the 7th District Regiment, which had signed up for thirty days, was about to be asked to enlist for the full three-year stretch. It had an incompetent colonel, was totally undisciplined, and had lost whatever morale it had ever had. Unless a good man took hold of the regiment at once there was not a chance that anybody would re-enlist. With their drinking and fighting and robbing of chicken roosts, the men were the scourge of central Illinois; worse yet, they were beginning to be known as "Governor Yates's Hellions."

Yates made Grant colonel of this regiment and awaited results.

He did not have to wait long. Grant took command on June 16, 1861. He had no uniform, and he was not an imposing sight. He wore a rusty civilian coat and an old felt hat, his shoulders were as always a little stooped, his beard looked as if it could stand a trim—and the wild young volunteers who had just gone through one colonel suspected gleefully that they were about to go through another. When Grant came out on the parade ground they hooted and jeered, and some went so far as to jostle him and give him the elbow.

And then suddenly they realized that they were wrong. The carefree roughneck days were over. They were not going to go through this colonel; they were going to do exactly what he told them to do, and in the end they were going to be soldiers. From now on there would be no more fooling around.

It is not altogether clear just how Grant did it. He did not invoke the terrible authority which the law gives a regimental commander in wartime, because he did not actually have it yet. The time of these men was about to expire, and nothing on earth could make them yield obedience if they did not feel like it. Grant just moved in and took charge and made them like it. Apparently there was something about the man. . . .

Earlier that spring, in Galena, a worthy captain of volunteers, trying without much luck to instruct his company in infantry drill, saw Grant looking on. Recognizing the former regular, he asked him to drill the company, handing over his sword and belt. Grant buckled on the equipment and stood facing the company, a stubby little storekeeper with a saber belted to his waist. Then he drew the blade, and it flashed in the sunlight — and, said the company's captain, there was suddenly an inexplicable transformation: this was the way you handled a sword, this was the way you took command of soldiers, and this man who never wanted to be an officer and always disliked soldiering was somehow very, very good at it.

Grant quickly had the 7th District Regiment in hand. It re-enlisted for the war, too. Here Grant got invaluable help from two prominent Democratic politicians, John A. McClernand and John A. Logan, who came in and orated to the men just before the decision was made. McClernand was known as an ardent Unionist, but Grant was a bit uneasy about Logan, who came from southern Illinois, where there seemed to be almost as many secessionists as in Virginia itself. But Logan came out strongly for the war and urged the men to sign up for the three-year pull; he was cheered wildly, and by the end of the day the men had re-enlisted and were formally in Federal service as the 21st Illinois Volunteers.

On July 3, when Grant took them over to Quincy on the Mississippi River, he remarked that the regiment was "in a good state of discipline" and noted that the men were "well up in company drill."

That move to Quincy helped with the discipline. Always before, troops went out from Springfield by train. When Grant got his orders he noticed that he had ten days to make the move, and he announced that the regiment would go on foot. It would take longer but there was plenty of time, and since the boys were going to do a power of cross-country hiking before the war ended they might as well get a little experience.

The first day the regiment marched five miles and camped, and Grant announced that the march would be resumed at six in the morning. Morning came, and six o'clock, and nobody was ready. Grant waited, and after an hour or so everybody had eaten and packed up, and at last the regiment moved. That night, as before, he announced that they would march at six A.M. At six the next morning, just as before, nobody was ready — but this time the colonel ordered the march to begin anyway. Half the men were left behind, scurrying about frantically to strike tents and pack gear, and the rest went stumbling down the road half dressed and unfed, carrying pants and shoes. After a couple of miles of this Grant called a halt, so that the men could finish dressing and the laggards could catch up.

That night, once again, he announced a six o'clock start for the next morning. And at six in the morning the whole regiment was fed, dressed, packed up, in line, and ready to go. And after a while they got to the river.

Grant had been in service three weeks and he had tamed the wild young men, and that was fine. What was much more significant, although nobody could appreciate it just then, was the simple fact that the government had U. S. Grant on the river, in command of troops, looking south. Far down under the surface, the war had begun to settle in the way it was to go.

The Mississippi was basic, in Western thinking. What happened in the East might or might not matter, but this river was the road to the world and the future, the inescapable geographic symbol of the fact that if the West would live and grow it must lie at the heart of a single undivided nation. The railway network was already replacing the river as a traffic artery, but that did not destroy the symbol. The river could be seen and felt, traditions had been built around it, men would fight for it and weave legends about their fighting, and they would make any sacrifice to keep this valley open.

This was instinctive. Grant doubtless reacted to it as automatically as Robert E. Lee reacted to his own instinctive feeling about Virginia. An articulate man like William T. Sherman might say that the valley was empire and that the side that won the river would win the war. Grant never talked about it, but the luck of the draw put him from the beginning where he could fight for it.

Grant's thinking, formulated in the arid years just before the war, had gone beyond the valley to embrace that other cardinal point in the Western attitude — the feeling that the Federal government was friend and not foe, the common man's champion, the means by which he could defend his rights. Because he saw it thus, Grant was enraged by the secession of Virginia, whereas South Carolina's act had only depressed him. For South Carolina, he wrote, there was much excuse, "for the last generation have been educated, from their infancy, to look upon their Government as oppressive and tyrannical and only to be endured until such time as they have sufficient strength to strike it down. Virginia and other border states have no such excuse."

After the war, he remarked that most Southerners should have had the Western viewpoint; they owned no slaves, had few advantages and lived in comparative poverty. They stood to gain by the triumph of the Federal government, he felt, "for they too needed emancipation."

Few Southerners saw it so in 1861, however, and Grant and the 21st Illinois campaigned across northeastern Missouri, marching a great deal (as Grant had foretold) and learning much. Once Grant took the men off to attack a Confederate camp in a lonely creek bottom, and he was oppressed by the responsibility. As he led the men up a hill beyond which he expected to meet the enemy, he was (he confessed afterward) badly scared and would have given anything to be back in Illinois. Yet when they topped the hill they found the enemy camp deserted. The Confederates had fled — and Grant realized that his opponent had been just as frightened as he himself had been. Always after that, before battle, he would remember: The other fellow is just as scared of me as I am of him.

Other lessons were more perplexing, for it seemed that this war was following some devious logic of its own. Grant at first believed that the South must presently see the hopelessness of its struggle and give up. Yet the secessionists were terribly dogged and tenacious and they might take a great deal of whipping. Grant was enforcing rules against forage and pillage, refusing to let his men enter even abandoned houses; the regiment was behaving much better now, in enemy country, than it had behaved in its native Illinois. Yet this seemed to win no friends, and in a letter to his sister Grant remarked on the perversity of Confederate civilians:

"Send Union troops among them and respect all their rights, pay for everything you get, and they become desperate and reckless because their state sovereignty is invaded. Troops of the opposite side march through and take everything they want, leaving no pay but scrip, and they become desperate Secession partisans because they have nothing more to lose. Every change makes them more desperate."

At Mexico, Missouri, guarding the line of the Hannibal and St. Joseph Railway, Grant learned that his old West Point friend Lyon, to whom he had vainly applied for a job a few months ago, had had a hot fight with Rebels at Wilson's Creek, in the southwestern part of the state, and had been killed in action. At about the same time Grant read in a St. Louis newspaper something that had a more direct personal impact: he himself had been promoted brigadier general of volunteers.

This happened partly because of the help of Grant's congressman, Elihu Washburne, and partly because of the quaint way in which the Washington government handed out commissions in those days. Washburne had met Grant at Galena, that spring, and had been impressed. (Another who had been impressed was a hot-blooded lawyer, John A. Rawlins, who was presently to join Grant's staff and be his right-hand man to the day of his death.) Early in August, Lincoln was about to create three dozen brigadiers, and since organizing an army seemed to be much like organizing a political machine — which, considering the kind of war they had got into, was not altogether illogical — Lincoln asked a number of good Union congress-men for recommendations. Washburne sent in Grant's name, and on August 7 the commission was issued. From now on he was General Grant.

Top command in Missouri then was held by the flamboyant "Pathfinder" of the West, Major General John C. Frémont. Frémont had been Republican candidate for President in 1856 — Grant was alleged to have quipped, later on, that he voted for Buchanan that year because he did not know Buchanan and did know Frémont — and although Frémont had much fame and the undying loyalty of the abolitionists he had almost no practical military capacity. He did, however, have strong notions about the importance of winning control of the Mississippi valley, and although he did not quite know how to go about doing it he at length took one step that led in the right direction. He put U. S. Grant in command at Cairo, Illinois, with control over southern Illinois and south-eastern Missouri.

Grant went to Cairo on September 4, in civilian clothes. He had given away his colonel's uniform when he was promoted, and his brigadier's uniform had not yet been delivered. He had a little trouble at first making the colonel commanding at Cairo understand that the plain citizen who had just walked in was the new general, taking charge. When that was put straight Grant set up head-quarters in a bank, sitting behind the cashier's window with clerks and aides all about him, conducting the military business of his district for all the world like a paying teller.

Not for long would he be bound to an office. The war was five months old, now, and it was beginning to approach the stage of action. In the East, the Bull Run fever had run its course, the Army of the Potomac was getting professional organization and training, and a powerful amphibious expedition to take seacoast bases and to seal off the Carolina sounds was being mounted. Brilliant young General McClellan was on his way up, and it was clear that he would soon replace Winfield Scott as commander of the Federal armies. In due time, a co-ordinated war plan would probably emerge.

Meanwhile, Cairo was a post of opportunity, and Grant recognized it the day after he took command.

Cairo is at the southern tip of Illinois, where the Ohio joins the Mississippi, and just across the Ohio is Kentucky. Kentucky was tragically divided in sentiment, half Unionist and half Confederate; it was not uncommon for one boy in a family to go north to enlist while his brother went south. The state had been trying frantically to preserve neutrality in this fratricidal war where neutrality was impossible. Federal and Confederate governments wooed Kentucky ardently, but so far they had respected its neutrality and had sent no troops across its borders.

On September 5 the Confederates jumped the gun. The order came from Major General Leonidas Polk, who had been graduated from West Point in 1827, had resigned from the army to study for the ministry and had become Episcopal bishop of Louisiana, as portly and dignified as any bishop need be. He had gone to Richmond to minister to Louisiana troops, and had urged Jefferson Davis to lose no time getting a good general out west to hold the Mississippi for the Confederacy. Apparently his argument was persuasive; Davis immediately made him a major general and sent him out to do the job.

Polk believed that if the Confederates did not enter Kentucky the Federals would. Union troops had been seen in Belmont, Missouri, across the river from the Kentucky city of Columbus, which was the northern terminus of the Mobile and Ohio Railway. These Federals, Polk suspected, would soon cross the river and take Columbus. To prevent it he marched troops up from Tennessee under Major General Gideon Pillow — the one Confederate soldier for whom Grant would ever express outright scorn — and occupied the place in strength. He planned to put big guns on the high bluff at Columbus, closing the river to Yankee steamboats.

Grant heard about this before the Kentucky authorities did. The governor was secessionist but a majority of the legislature was for the Union, and Grant immediately telegraphed the speaker of the Kentucky House of Representatives, telling him what had happened. He then sent a wire to General Frémont at St. Louis, announcing that unless he was forbidden he would go up the Ohio and occupy the Kentucky city of Paducah.

Paducah was of high strategic importance. Thirty miles east of Cairo, by land, it lay at the mouth of the Tennessee River, a navigable waterway straight across Kentucky and Tennessee into the deep South. If the North proposed to open the Mississippi, Paducah was a place it had to have.

Grant heard nothing from Frémont, which was just what he had been hoping for, and that night he began to move. Cairo was a naval base as well as an army district command headquarters, and at the wharves lay the gunboats *Tyler, Lexington* and *Conestoga* — converted river steamers, unarmored but well armed, potentially very useful, especially on a river where the enemy had no warships at all. With these ships as escort, Grant embarked two regiments of infantry and a battery of artillery, and on the morning of September 6 he occupied Paducah. Leaving troops and gunboats to hold the place, he hurried back to Cairo, where he found a telegram from Frémont telling him he might take Paducah if he thought that he was strong enough. He then got another wire, reprimanding him for carrying on an unauthorized correspondence with the speaker of the Kentucky House of Representatives, and after that he got a third message saying that Brigadier General Charles F. Smith was being sent down to take command at Paducah independently of Grant.

His action had been upheld, but he had drawn two rebukes. Yet the rebukes did not matter much. The campaign to open the Mississippi Valley was under way.

2. *Unconditional Surrender*

THE OCCUPATION of Columbus and Paducah changed everything. Until then, the war in the West had seemed chiefly a matter of Missouri. Now the emphasis shifted. Grant was no more than back in Cairo before he was asking permission to go down and take Columbus away from Gideon Pillow.

Permission was denied. Matters were going badly in Missouri, and Frémont was too busy to pay much attention to Kentucky. Yet as weeks passed the vital importance of the Cairo district began to make itself felt. Bit by bit, Grant's strength was increased. Paducah was put under his command again, its garrison raised to seven thousand men. By midautumn Grant had, in all, some twenty thousand soldiers in his district.

On the Confederate side, too, Kentucky was getting more attention. For supreme command in the West the Richmond government sent out General Albert Sidney Johnston, whom some considered the Confederacy's best soldier. Before long he would get the romantic P. G. T. Beauregard as second in command. Johnston drew an east-west line across Kentucky, with Columbus as its western anchor and with its eastern terminus in the upland country north of Cumberland Gap. In the center, under the Simon Buckner who had once loaned Grant money to pay a hotel bill, a strong force held Bowling Green and sent expeditions north and northeast to cut communications and alarm the Yankees.

Grant's command became more active. Forts were built on the Kentucky side of the Ohio, armed reconnaissances were made, and if nothing much came of these movements the soldiers at least got a little experience — as did the brigadier general commanding them. In addition, Grant got an insight into the possibilities of amphibious warfare. The navy was building ironclads and would soon add them to the flotilla based at Cairo. In command was Flag Officer Andrew Foote, a salty character with an engaging fringe of whiskers around a block-of-oak face, who had fully as much aggressiveness in his system as Grant. The two men understood each other, and looked forward to action.

When the action came it was rather pointless but very spirited. Armed Confederates had been rampaging about in southern Missouri, and Grant sent troops down from Cape Girardeau to attend to them. To protect these troops against interference from the big Confederate base at Columbus, Grant put five regiments on transports and, with Foote's wooden gunboats for escort, dropped down the Mississippi on November 6 to see what could be done.

Across the river from Columbus was the hamlet of Belmont. The Union troops whose presence there had originally provoked Polk into invading Kentucky were long since gone, and Confederates were camped there now. Belmont seems not to have figured in anyone's calculations when the Federal troops were embarked, but as they cruised downstream Grant saw that officers and men were all keyed up at the prospect of action and he felt that morale would suffer if they went back to Cairo without doing anything. On the morning of November 7 he pulled up to the Missouri shore a few miles above Belmont, disembarked some twenty-five hundred infantry, and marched down to assail the Rebel camp.

He made the assault somewhat inexpertly, as was perhaps natural for a general leading men into battle for the first time. He put all of his troops in line, with no reserve held back for emergencies. But General Pillow, who commanded at Belmont, was even less expert, and instead of holding his men in camp to await the attack he valiantly sent them out to meet the Yankees head on. A sharp fight resulted and the Confederates were routed, fleeing in disorder to the shelter of the river bank downstream. Grant's men had a high time looting the Confederate camp.

Grant's big mistake was that he did not hold some troops in hand, in case the Rebels should revive and try to renew the battle. After a while the Confederates over in Columbus recovered their wits and sent reinforcements across to make a new fight. The Federals then found themselves in a bad fix. Most of the soldiers were still rampaging about the captured camp, and Foote's unarmored gunboats could not come down to help because of those heavy guns on the bluffs across the river. The victory suddenly turned into defeat, with the Unionists running upstream for their transports, pursued by jubilant Rebels. In the end Grant got all his men aboard, embarking himself last of all, and the expedition went back to Cairo.

Grant had lost 485 men, with about 125 of his wounded falling into the hands of Confederates. Rebel losses apparently were about equal; in addition, their camp had been looted, and Grant's men had carried off two field-pieces and had spiked four more. To balance that, the Federals had had to flee in disorder, and if they had planned to seize a foothold from which they could bombard Columbus (as the Confederates supposed) they had unquestionably failed. The Confederates published it as a victory, and most Northerners agreed.

But Grant's soldiers felt that they had done a big thing. They had fought a hard battle and they had made their foes run away; they had captured a Rebel camp, and they had tangible souvenirs to show for it. On the whole they were chesty about it all, and they were convinced that their General Grant was quite a man.

More important, this fight indicated that the Federals along the river were going to be aggressive.

So far the period of watchful waiting in the Kentucky area had not really ended, even though each side had moved troops into the state. The Union commander in Kentucky had originally been General Robert Anderson, of Fort Sumter fame, but his health had failed and he had been replaced by William T. Sherman. Sherman was going through a strange phase just then, crediting the Confederates with more soldiers and more aggressive intentions than they actually had, and behaving with a worried caution very uncharacteristic of the Sherman of later years. In the Virginia theater the Federal authorities had been showing a genius for stalemate, and the same business had been developing here in the West. But now things were beginning to move, and the attention of the Union high command was inexorably drawn to the operations around Cairo.

The Union high command by now was young General McClellan, Scott having at last been shelved for age. Frémont also had been removed from St. Louis, his place taken by Henry Wager Halleck — "Old Brains" to the officer corps, a man who had written military texts and was believed to be a learned strategist. Sherman himself had come under a cloud so black that newspaper critics were calling him insane; he was replaced by General Don Carlos Buell, a close friend of McClellan's and, in the general estimation of the War Department, a man of equal promise.

McClellan, Halleck and Buell, then, were the new team, and that hackneyed word "brilliant" was applied to all three. The Administration expected much of them. It had yet to learn what brilliance can look like when it is watered down by excessive caution and a distaste for making decisions, and when it is accompanied every step of the way by a strong prima donna complex.

The year 1861 ended with an air of vast preparation but with nothing much actually in motion. At Cairo, Grant got on with the training and equipment of his growing command. He also quietly demonstrated that his district was not to be a happy hunting ground for shady contractors and speculators, although he had to risk his official neck to do it.

These characters were making a very good thing out of the war, selling grain and forage to army quartermasters at prices far above the market. Grant caught on, canceled contracts wholesale, and refused to let government money be paid out in his district on contracts that had been approved over his head in St. Louis. He learned a great deal about the way bids were rigged, and about secret understandings by which supposedly competing contractors were working in cahoots; and he cracked down hard, striking some rather important knuckles as he did so.

There came to see him, one day, Leonard Swett, one of the most prominent lawyers in Illinois and a Republican politician of note; he was, in fact, the man who had put Lincoln's name in nomination at the 1860 convention, and he was close to the President personally and politically. Grant was warned bluntly that Swett and the contractors he represented had influence enough to remove any general who made a nuisance of himself.

Swett threatened to go to the President if Grant kept on canceling contracts. Grant told him to go right ahead; meanwhile he, Grant, would continue to buy materials in the open market at prices substantially under those of the Swett contractors. If necessary, he would seize the Illinois Central Railroad (in which Swett was a big stockholder) in order to move the goods to camp. Further, if he found Swett in his military district after twenty-four hours he would throw him neck and heels into a military prison. Come to think of it, he would shoot him.

That ended that. Long afterward, it developed that

Swett did in fact go to Lincoln with the whole story, including Grant's threat. By that time Lincoln had begun to get a little of Grant's essential flavor. As Swett himself told the story, Lincoln warned him that he had better stay out of Cairo, because if Grant was threatening to shoot him he was just the sort of man to go ahead and do it.

In any case, Grant's fight for honest contracts was not undercut from Washington.

Early in January, 1862, it began to be clear that the time for military action was very near.

From the Confederate fortress at Columbus to the center of Albert Sidney Johnston's defensive line at Bowling Green the distance was about a hundred and forty miles, air line. Halfway between these points the Tennessee and Cumberland rivers, here parallel and only twelve miles apart, crossed the Tennessee–Kentucky border. Since they were an obvious channel of invasion, the Confederates had built forts just south of the state line to bar the way to Yankee steamers. On the Cumberland, the more easterly of the two rivers, flowing down from Nashville, the capital of Tennessee, was Fort Donelson, a work of considerable strength. Over on the Tennessee was Fort Henry, built on low ground that was subject to flooding, considered very frail by its garrison. Across the Tennessee the Rebels were building another work, Fort Heiman, to make good Fort Henry's deficiencies.

As 1862 began it became evident that General Buckner, commanding Confederates at Bowling Green, was being reinforced. Buell wanted to move against him, but felt that he could do so only if Halleck kept the Rebels busy at the western end of the line, and much correspondence passed between McClellan, Buell and Halleck on this matter. The correspondence eventually roused Halleck a bit, and on January 6 he ordered Grant to make a demonstration toward Fort Henry in order to delude the Rebels and make them think that it was there, and not at Bowling Green, that a blow was likely to fall.

Grant's demonstration was only a feint, but while he was making it he cruised up the Tennessee with Foote and watched the navy exchange a few long-range salvos with Fort Henry. This did the Confederacy no direct harm, but it did reveal to Grant and Foote the extreme weakness of the place. After he got back to Cairo, Grant learned that the Tennessee was rising and that part of Fort Henry was under water. He hurried to St. Louis and asked Halleck to let him make a real attack.

Halleck refused, and snubbed him hard. Grant wrote afterward that he was "received with so little cordiality" that he presented his case poorly, and that Halleck quickly cut him short "as if my plan was preposterous." Crestfallen, Grant returned to Cairo.

However, he was not giving up. Before January ended, he and Foote united in a new request. This time Grant said flatly that he could take and hold Fort Henry, and this time he got a better reception.

Far over in eastern Kentucky, Federal General George H. Thomas had just defeated Confederate General Felix K. Zollicoffer, opening a road into eastern Tennessee, where Lincoln greatly wanted to send a Federal army. Thomas was under Buell, and if this success was followed up it would be Buell rather than Halleck who would get credit for breaking the Confederate line and who would thus become top dog in the West. Furthermore, Halleck had just been told (erroneously) that Beauregard, who was coming West to join Johnston, was bringing heavy re-inforcements, and if any blows were to be struck it appeared that they had better be struck before those reinforcements arrived.

For these reasons, Grant's proposed smash at Fort Henry looked better than it had earlier. Rather to his surprise, Grant on February 1 got authorization to make the move.

He set out with fifteen thousand men, in two divisions. One was commanded by the John McClernand who had helped talk the 21st Illinois into enlisting for three years — a brigadier now, full of ardor, ambition and political influence. The other was led by Charles F. Smith, who had been commandant of cadets when Grant was at West Point — a ramrod-straight officer with flaring mustachios, the very beau ideal of the old-army regular officer. Both Grant and Sherman were to confess that they always felt very junior and humble in his presence, as if they were still cadets, although by now both ranked him.

The move to Fort Henry took longer than Grant had anticipated. There were not enough transports and the troops had to go in relays, and as this was by far the largest army for which Grant had ever been responsible — it was actually bigger than the army Scott had taken to Mexico City — he still had much to learn about logistics. It was February 5 before he had his men ashore below the Confederate fort, and he was not ready to attack until the next day. Then he sent Smith and his division up the west bank to take Fort Heiman, took McClernand's division along the east bank to seize Fort Henry itself, and had Foote move his gunboats up river to soften the place with a bombardment.

The Rebel defense caved in with embarrassing suddenness. The Southern commander had no intention of making a real stand here, as Fort Heiman was only half finished and Fort Henry was only half above water, and he sent most of his men over to Fort Donelson as soon as the Yankees appeared. He stood up to the bombardment bravely enough, but he was badly overmatched and before long, with several guns dismounted, he hauled down his flag — surrendering, in point of fact, to the navy, Grant's column not yet having arrived. But Foote and Grant were good friends; interservice rivalry was kept within bounds, and Grant telegraphed the news to Halleck.

He added, quite unexpectedly, that he would go over and capture Fort Donelson on February 8.

As it turned out he was entirely too optimistic, and his telegram contained a thumping underestimate of the time that would be needed. Rain and snow were clogging the roads, Fort Donelson was ever so much stronger than Fort Henry, and the Confederates were reinforcing it so heavily that when Grant got his army over there he would actually be outnumbered. But the effect of Grant's telegram — on Halleck, on Buell and on far-off McClellan — was electric.

These three had been planning an offensive against Johnston's army, but they had not been able to agree about it. Not one of the trio could reach a decision quickly or move fast after he had done so. Halleck and Buell were darkly suspicious of each other, and everybody was thinking hard of the personal advantage which could be won in the coming campaign. McClellan tended to favor his friend Buell, but he was too far away and too busy with plans for his own campaign in Virginia to give much attention to Kentucky.

Now, suddenly, in the midst of their leisurely tele-
graphic weighing of pros and cons, the balance was vio-
lently upset by this subordinate of Halleck's who had gone
ahead and acted and who was threatening to act even further.

Scenting an advantage, Halleck called loudly for reinforcements and more authority. Buell, suspecting that he
was being outmaneuvered in the struggle for power, tried
to co-operate but could get no statements of Halleck's
plans — which was natural, because Halleck hardly had
any; he had only that telegram saying that Grant was about
to attack Fort Donelson. McClellan suggested that perhaps
Buell had better go to Fort Donelson in person — in which
case, since he ranked Grant, he would take command. Halleck suggested that some of Buell's troops be sent, and
said that he himself would go to the scene of action. (He
ranked Buell, and if they were both there Buell would be
under his command.) Then a new idea developed: perhaps Buell could take his men up the Cumberland while
Halleck took his up the Tennessee. That raised problems,
because the navy did not yet have enough gunboats to con-
voy simultaneous expeditions on both rivers.

This might easily have gone on for months — all three
generals were masters at this sort of disputation — except
that on February 17 another telegram came to Halleck
from General Grant. Fort Donelson had surrendered, with
approximately fifteen thousand prisoners of war.

It had not been easy. The navy had suffered heavily,
losing men and seeing its new ironclads disabled. A sally
by Confederate defenders had knocked McClernand's division aside and had briefly opened a way of escape, if
the defenders wanted one. Inexperienced Federal sol-

diers who had discarded blankets and overcoats because it was a nuisance to carry them had to sleep in the snow, in below-freezing temperatures, without fires.

But reinforcements had come up, and the hole in the line had been plugged before the Rebels could do anything about it. General Smith had broken the Confederate line, leading his green troops in a hot charge through dense thickets and up the side of a wooded ravine. By the end of the second day of the fighting it was clear that the jig was up. The two ranking Confederate officers — John B. Floyd, who had been Secretary of War in Buchanan's cabinet, and the General Pillow whom Grant despised so much — slipped away to safety by night, and Nathan Bedford Forrest got the Confederate cavalry out. Left in command was Grant's old friend Buckner, and next morning Buckner surrendered the fort and everybody in it.

He was a little bitter. When he sent out a white flag, suggesting a parley on terms of surrender, Grant gave him a curt note saying there could be no terms except unconditional surrender, adding that he proposed to attack at once. Buckner considered this unchivalrous and ungenerous, but there was no help for it.

Halleck was jubilant, for Grant was under his command and so Grant's triumph was his triumph. He relayed the news to Washington and asked that he be given top command in the West: "I ask this in return for Forts Henry and Donelson." He also suggested that Buell, Grant and John Pope (who commanded troops working their way down the Mississippi) be made major generals. A bit later he urged that Smith also be promoted, saying that Grant's victory was really due to him. Magnanimously, he invited Buell to "come down to the Cumberland and take command," telling him that the decisive battle of the West would be fought soon and that Buell ought to be in it as second in command — under Halleck, naturally.

It was not going to go quite that way.

Back in Washington, Abraham Lincoln had been watching the whole business with a canny scrutiny that overlooked very little; and he had his own ideas about who ought to be rewarded for what. To the Senate, Lincoln sent just one name for promotion — Ulysses S. Grant, to be major general of volunteers. The Senate at once voted confirmation. The dull plodder on whom Halleck, McClellan and Buell all looked down had after all been the actual author of victory.

3. Turning Point

It was a big thing that had happened, and it changed the entire war.

Northern morale had been low; now it went up into the clouds. The chain of defeats was snapped. Here was a clear-cut, decisive victory, with a Federal army penning its antagonist up inside fortified lines, waging furious two-day battle at the cost of twenty-eight hundred casualties, and then moving in to sweep the board clean. Never before on the continent had so many prisoners of war been taken in one engagement.

Grant's note to Buckner caught men's imagination. It had an exultant, Star-Spangled, Yankee Doodle ring to it — put up or shut up, fight or quit, this thing is not going to stop until one or the other of us cannot get up off the floor. Perhaps the shortest way out of the war was the way that led straight on through; people who had hardly heard of U. S. Grant before now began to discover with delight that his very initials stood for the words of triumph — Unconditional Surrender.

The general himself soon learned that fame in America can have some unexpected by-products. He had been a dutiful pipe smoker — an associate remembered that at Cairo, Grant was usually pulling at an imposing meerschaum with a curved stem ten inches long — but when he left Foote's gunboats at Donelson to gallop to the scene of McClernand's repulse, he took a cigar which Foote offered him, stuck it unlit in his mouth, forgot about it, and rode through the rest of the battle with it. Newspaper stories told how he was always to be seen, when in action, with a cigar in his mouth, and admirers back home did the rest; Grant soon got enough boxes of cigars to fumigate a whole brigade. Most of these were very good cigars, it seemed a shame to waste them — and before long Grant was a confirmed cigar smoker, usually carrying as many as two dozen in his pockets when he began the day's routine.

In sober fact the Donelson victory was just as big as elated Northerners believed. It cracked the Confederacy's hold on the West, once and for all, and left Johnston badly crippled. (Neither he nor any other Confederate general could afford the loss of sixteen-thousand odd soldiers at one blow.) It compelled him to abandon Nashville at once and, within a few days, the fortress at Columbus. It paved the way for the Federal capture of the Confederate fort on Island Number Ten in the Mississippi, led to the fall of Memphis, and finally caused Johnston to pull his troops all the way back to the State of Mississippi. Kentucky was hopelessly lost to the Confederacy now, and Tennessee, one of its most populous and important states, was in little better case. In all the war few battles had consequences as far-reaching as this one.

Then and later, Grant believed that the whole war might have been won in that year if the victory at Donelson had been properly followed up. Instead, he remarked, the stunned Confederates were given time to recruit their armies and to fortify their new positions. The follow-up was lacking because the Federals did not have unified command in the West.

Halleck at least believed in unified command, and he kept bombarding Washington with telegrams demanding it — for himself. He was not getting it just then, however. Instead he was tartly told to get on with the war and to let the government worry about unification. Growing morose, Halleck took it out on Grant, who was getting too much of the glory anyway. To McClellan he sent a long bill of complaint, alleging that Grant sent him no reports, ignored his orders and did not answer his telegrams, and declaring that Grant's army was as badly demoralized by its victory as the eastern army had been by the defeat at Bull Run. Wearily and self-righteously, Halleck concluded: "I am worn out and tired with this neglect and inefficiency."

When McClellan made the natural reply — if things are that bad, put the man under arrest — Halleck shifted his position. He did not really think it necessary to arrest Grant, but he felt obliged to report that he had heard that "Grant has resumed his former habits." To anyone familiar with the old army gossip, that of course could mean but one thing: Grant was off on a big drunk.

This was a monstrous untruth, whether Halleck actually believed it or not. Whatever Grant may have done at other times, he was cold sober now. He was spending a good part of his time answering heckling messages from Halleck, who needled him daily with an infinite number of petty complaints. Grant did his best to make proper reply. (One trouble, it came out later, was a simple mix-up in the message center: certain telegrams between the generals had just never been delivered.) He also requested that he be relieved of his command "until I can be placed right in the estimation of those higher in authority."

Then, just as the breach seemed past mending, there came unexpected healing.

The War Department reshuffled its command, demoting McClellan and giving Halleck what he had been angling for, top command in the West. Also, it ordered Halleck ("by direction of the President") to make formal report on just what military sins Grant had committed. In effect, Halleck was told that he must either prepare formal charges and make them stick, or get Grant out from under the cloud which Halleck's own dispatches had created.

With the big prize in his hands, Halleck was in much better humor. Also, it was impossible to prepare formal charges because there was no real substance to any of his complaints. A facile letter writer, Halleck explained to the War Department that the whole trouble in respect to Grant had been due to misunderstandings that now, happily, were cleared up; that if any irregularities had existed they had been remedied; that if Grant had erred anywhere it had been through excess of zeal — and, to come to an end of it, that the whole business had best be forgotten.

Soothing Grant was something else again, but Halleck did his best. He wrote Grant a carefully worded letter in which he spoke in large terms about misunderstandings, and he explained that Grant would not be relieved of his command. Instead: "I wish you as soon as your new army is in the field to assume the immediate command and lead it on to new victories." He also led Grant to believe that most of the trouble had been provoked by McClellan.

With an active campaign about to begin, Grant dropped his request to be relieved and buckled down to work.

The Confederates were concentrating at the railroad junction town of Corinth, Mississippi. Grant wanted to go for them at once; he had a substantial army now, six divisions of infantry with a total strength of perhaps forty thousand men. The Confederates had just about that number at Corinth, but Grant was confident — perhaps a little too confident — that in a stand-up fight against equal numbers his men would win.

Halleck agreed that Corinth was the objective, but he wanted a strong numerical advantage. He proposed therefore to bring together on the Tennessee River the armies of Grant and Buell. He would then come to the scene himself to take top command, and the united force would move on Johnston. Grant was told to wait at some suitable point on the river while Buell brought his army over from Nashville.

As March came to an end, Grant had his men in camp

at Pittsburg Landing on the Tennessee. Five divisions were drawn up side by side, facing south, near a country chapel known as Shiloh Church. The sixth, under Lew Wallace, lay in support, half a dozen miles downstream. Grant himself had headquarters at the town of Savannah, across the river and below, the most likely point for Buell's men to reach on their hike from Nashville. The camp at Shiloh was in command of General Smith. When Smith fell ill — an illness which was to cost him his life — general control of the forward zone passed to Sherman, who had just joined Grant's army as a division commander. Between Grant and Sherman an enduring and momentous friendship was forming.

In planning the move on Corinth, Halleck and Grant and all the other Union generals made one small error. They assumed that the Confederates would sit still and wait to be attacked.

Corinth was about twenty miles from Shiloh Church. Johnston and Beauregard had vexing problems of organization, discipline and supply for an army of enthusiastic but largely untrained soldiers, and they knew as well as anyone that if they waited where they were and let Halleck's combined forces descend on them they would be mashed. The one hope was to jump the gun and smite the Yankees before the separate pieces of Halleck's host could unite. Grant's was the nearer army and hence the logical target. Early in April, therefore, the Confederates took to the road for Shiloh.

The march was the next thing to a complete fiasco. Progress was miserably slow; soldiers straggled, fired their muskets, whooped and yelled and frolicked; and Beauregard, at last, wanted to call everything off and go back to

Corinth. By no possible chance, he argued, could the Yankees be ignorant of a movement as clumsy and as noisy as this one.

Beauregard ought to have been right, but he was wrong. The Federals were well aware that numerous Rebels were moving about in the wooded country beyond the Yankee picket lines, but it was believed that these must be scouts, roving cavalry, foraging details or something similar. Grant looked for an attack on his outposts, to be sure; he believed that Lew Wallace, isolated downstream, might be molested, and he arranged with Sherman to send help quickly in case Wallace should need it. But he apparently never imagined that Johnston would come up from Corinth with his entire army and risk everything in a head-on attack. For the last time in the war, Grant failed to credit an adversary with the drive and daring he himself would have shown in a similar position.

So Beauregard was wrong, in spite of logic. Johnston overruled him, and in the quiet dawn of Sunday, April 6, 1862, he massed his army in three successive lines and drove them in through the woods to attack the Yankees.

One of the bloodiest and most tragic battles of the war followed — a singular milestone in American history, illuminating as does no other battle the amazing courage and pugnacity of the Northern and Southern soldiers of the Civil War. Most of the men who fought at Shiloh had never fought before. Their discipline was very sketchy, regimental officers knew very little more than enlisted men, the higher commanders were just learning their grim trade. The Northerners were not entrenched — professional soldiers at that time felt that it ruined morale to have the men dig ditches — and they had to receive the attack just as they had camped. The Southerners were put into action inexpertly, in a formation that destroyed most lines of authority and doomed divisions and brigades to get completely intermingled. It would not have been surprising if both armies had turned and fled after half an hour of it. Instead they stayed and fought for two days — and the entire war had no fighting more terrible than the fighting which took place here.

There were perhaps thirty-three thousand Federal soldiers present when the battle began. Some were ground under at the first onset, and others picked up their heels and made for the rear without delay; at the river bank from five to ten thousand paralyzed fugitives were cowering all day, and Grant said later that at no time after the battle got well under way did he have as many as twenty-five thousand men in line. But those twenty-five thousand stuck it out, and an appalling number of them got shot. . . . Union and Confederate officers agreed afterward that Shiloh proved one singular fact about the untrained volunteer: if he was going to run at all, he would probably run during the first half hour. If he stuck past the first shock he would stick to the end.

Grant was at Savannah, five or six miles downstream, when the fighting began. Buell's advance guard was expected at any moment, and Grant left word for it to get up to Pittsburg Landing with all speed. He sent Lew Wallace orders to get his division to the scene of action by a forced march. (Wallace tried, but somehow he got on a wrong road, marched vigorously all day to no purpose, and reached the battlefield only after dark.) Then Grant hurried to Pittsburg Landing by steamer. went to the front, and did what he could to keep his sagging battle line from coming completely apart.

The Confederate attack drove the Federals almost back to the river, capturing their camps and many prisoners, and all day the Southerners seemed to be right on the edge of conclusive victory. Some of the deadliest fighting of the war took place in "the hornets' nest," a tangle of briars and scrub timber, where the greater part of a Federal division was captured. Leading his men in a charge here, Johnston was shot and killed; and here and elsewhere the Federals held on just long enough to avert disaster. Toward dusk Grant massed guns on a final height near the river. Union gunboats placed themselves where they could enfilade the Rebel line with large-caliber shell. Buell got to the scene, at the head of fresh troops. The Confederate drive slackened from sheer exhaustion, darkness came down at last, and the Federal lines held.

Next day Lew Wallace was up, and more of Buell's troops, and Grant had been able to do a little reorganizing. The battle began all over again. For half a day the men fought at the same furious pitch as in the first day's fighting. Then Yankee manpower began to tell, the Confederate lines were bent back, and finally Beauregard did the only thing that was left to him and ordered a retreat. The Confederate army went trailing back to Corinth, pursued briefly and without enthusiasm by weary Federals. Grant's men reoccupied their former camps, and it was time to make a count of losses and consider what to do next.

Losses had been almost incredible. In killed, wounded and missing the Federals had lost more than thirteen thousand men, most of them on the first day. Confederate losses may have been somewhat lower — certainly they lost fewer men captured — but they ran above twenty-five per cent of the total brought to the field. That newly organized, largely inexperienced armies could stand such losses without breaking in wild rout is still almost beyond belief, three generations later. The generals in the Civil War, whatever else may have been true of them, commanded human material as good as any armies ever had.

Indeed, in the real sense of the word these were not armies that fought at Shiloh. They were simply huge assemblies of citizens, thrown into an enormous combat and left to fight their way out of it. A Confederate brigadier confessed afterward that until the battle began he had never so much as seen a man fire a musket, and his comment — "We were all tyros: generals, colonels, captains, soldiers" — applied very largely to both sides.

Shiloh led to bitter recriminations. Northerners who ran away and were denounced for it back home defended themselves by exaggerating the extent to which their army had been taken by surprise. If evil things had happened they were all Grant's fault; and since some of these men had prominence and political power their complaints got a wide hearing. Old gossip was revived, and once again it was whispered (falsely) that Grant had been drunk. The fame won at Donelson was perceptibly dimmed. He was pictured now as a clumsy butcher. The fearful casualty lists, by far the worst that Americans had ever had to look at, laid gloom all across the land. The Southerner who said that New Orleans "had never really been glad again" after Shiloh summed it up for both sides.

Yet it is possible to overstate the criticism which descended on Grant. He had able defenders. Congressman

Washburne effectively argued his cause in Washington. General Sherman upheld him and bitterly denounced his critics, in a flood of letters that were widely circulated. Stories of how Grant had behaved during the battle were told with admiration. When Buell reached the scene, late on that dreadful first day, it was related, he scented disaster and asked Grant what on earth he would do if he had to retreat — there were not boats enough to get ten thousand men back across the river. Grimly, Grant replied that if he finally did retreat, ten thousand men would be all he would need transportation for. When all the criticisms had been voiced, one saving fact did remain: this general had stubbornly refused to admit defeat, and in the end he had won a victory.

A negative victory, to be sure. The enemy had attacked, had been beaten back, and at last had gone away. Yet the victory had effects that reached much farther than men then could see.

Donelson had broken the line and knocked the Confederate defenders clear back to the deep South. Shiloh had been the counterblow, the last chance to keep the Federals from applying superior strength to the remorseless advance that in the end would deprive the confederacy of the Mississippi and all the West and doom it to final defeat. The counterblow had failed. The odds against Confederate victory in the West, long enough to begin with, now became immeasurably longer. In the Eastern theater the campaigning had hardly got under way, but in the West a great turning point had been reached and passed.

4. *Hour of Decision*

GENERAL HALLECK was at the front now, operating as a field commander for the first and only time in
the war. He got to Shiloh on April 11, and he planned to
resume the old project for driving the Rebels out of Corinth. He would not move, however, until he had everything well in hand. The offensive would be conducted
with overwhelming force and with profound caution.
Nothing would be left to chance. There would be no
more surprises — not of Federals, nor for that matter of
Confederates either.

By the end of April, Halleck had assembled a hundred
and twenty thousand soldiers, a blend of three previously
independent armies — Grant's and Buell's, plus Pope's,
which had been brought over from the Mississippi after
the collapse of the Confederate system of forts running
upstream from Memphis. Grant, Buell and Pope were
rated as wing commanders, under Halleck as general in
chief, and on April 30 the vast army began to move.

It moved like a glacier, irresistibly but very slowly,
plowing up the countryside as it went. Every camp was entrenched as thoroughly as if it were to be held all year
against superior numbers. If there had been trouble at
Shiloh because the army was not dug in, that trouble
would never recur. In all the war, no army ever moved on
the enemy with such extreme deliberation — not even Mc-
Clellan's Army of the Potomac, which right at this time
was creeping up the Virginia peninsula from Yorktown.
Less than a mile a day was the average for Halleck's army,
and it was May 30 before the ponderous war machine was

at last drawn up before Corinth. It fortified its long front with great care, and Halleck told his generals that "there is every indication that the enemy will attack our left this morning."

That was the last thing the enemy was thinking about. The Confederate authorities had been trying hard to reorganize and reinforce the army that had fought at Shiloh, and although they had accomplished a good deal (and very grateful they were for the long respite Halleck had given them) they were still outnumbered more than two to one. An attack on Halleck's lines was simply out of the question.

All Beauregard asked, for the moment, was to get away unhurt, and while Halleck awaited attack Beauregard saw and accepted his chance. Keeping switch engines puffing and tooting, and ordering details to cheer periodically, so as to make the Yankees think trainloads of new recruits were arriving, he got his men and matériel out of town, dropped back to Tupelo, forty-five miles to the south, and left Halleck to occupy deserted Corinth at his leisure. When his departure was at last discovered, the Federals came in and immediately began to build a ring of fortifications around the little town.

Grant had been having a dismal time. From command of one wing of the army he had been kicked upstairs, to the post of second in command for the entire army. He quickly learned that this job was like that of Vice-President of the United States: it carried much honor and certain dim potentialities, but there was nothing whatever for the man who held it to do. He was a complete figurehead. The one time he ventured to make a suggestion — he proposed a sudden attack on Beauregard's flank, shortly before the arrival at Corinth — Halleck squelched him. Grant grew depressed, and applied at last for a thirty-day furlough — which, under the circumstances, would practically amount to taking himself out of the army for good.

Sherman heard about Grant's intention. In the heat of the fires at Shiloh, Sherman had acquired a tremendous admiration for Grant. Better than anyone else, he knew how the sheer force of Grant's will had kept Shiloh from becoming an overwhelming defeat. He was determined now that the man should not leave the army. He went to Grant's tent, pleaded with him, finally got him to withdraw the application for leave. Sooner or later, said Sherman, there would be a turn for the better.

Meanwhile, what little momentum Halleck's army had ever had in its invasion of the South had been lost. Halleck became entirely defense-minded. He would hold Corinth, which seemed to be a strategic spot. He would also hold Tennessee, and Buell was told to take his troops over to Chattanooga, repairing the Memphis and Chattanooga Railroad as he went. He would hold Memphis, and he sent Grant to take command there. He would hold other places, here and there; and presently his huge army was broken up, a bit of it here and another bit there, no single piece large enough to take the offensive. If the Confederates had failed to redeem Donelson at Shiloh, something very like another chance was being offered them.

Then fragmentation became complete. Washington called Halleck to the East, to take the vacant post of general in chief which McClellan had once held, and no replacement for Halleck in the West was named. The armies which he had scattered were no longer under a central command. Buell and Grant were again independent army commanders.

For Grant had come back to army command. He had been restored, that is, to the post he had held before Shiloh — command of western Tennessee and the territory north of it, plus as much of Mississippi as he might be able to get. On July 17, 1862, Halleck left for the East — where McClellan's army sweltered in a gloomy camp by the James River, recuperating from the defeat of the Seven Days — and Grant went down to Corinth to assume his new duties.

These were a trifle baffling. Under him were nine divisions of infantry, plus artillery and cavalry — and an immense area to hold, running all the way north to Cairo. The Tennessee River was at low-water stage and could not be relied on for transport. That meant all the railroads must be guarded, which called for two full divisions of troops. Two more divisions had to be held in Memphis, where Grant put Sherman in command. The main striking force, assembled in and around Corinth, thus was of moderate size. Until Grant either got more men or new orders, there was little he could do but sit tight and watch the foe.

The foe needed watching, this summer. Beauregard had been replaced by General Braxton Bragg, who was as baffling a mixture of high ability and sheer incompetence as the Confederacy could produce. Bragg had taken advantage of Buell's slow progress toward Chattanooga to go knifing up through middle Tennessee toward the Ohio River, his chief mission being to regain Kentucky for the South and to disrupt the Yankees' war plans as much as possible.

In the end, Bragg failed. He outmaneuvered Buell so thoroughly that Washington finally removed that officer from command, but Bragg was hopelessly unable to take advantage of his opportunities, and in the end he threw in what had looked like a winning hand and drifted back into central Tennessee. That did not happen until fall, however, and before it happened there was a period when the Union cause looked worse than at any time since the war began.

For Bragg was in Kentucky, just as if Donelson and Shiloh had been canceled out, and Lee was taking an army of invasion into Maryland, all Federal offensives in Virginia having collapsed; and down in Mississippi, Grant was getting his share of the backwash of Bragg's offensive.

When Bragg went north, Grant had to send troops to strengthen Buell, and his force at Corinth was whittled thin. A small but tough Confederate army under Earl Van Dorn and Sterling Price came up to chase him out of Mississippi. After an indecisive brush at Iuka, this force swung in to attack Corinth itself.

Grant's troops there were under hearty, red-faced General William S. Rosecrans, erratic and overexcitable but a stout fighter, and they broke the Confederate attack with heavy casualties and sent Van Dorn and Price off in headlong flight. Grant complained that Rosecrans did not follow up his victory — this Confederate army might have been destroyed outright if it had been pressed hard — but at least the threat to the Union grip on Mississippi was ended. Also, Lee was beaten in Maryland, Bragg fled south from Kentucky, and one more of this war's ever-recurring crises had been passed.

But if nothing had been lost, this summer of 1862,

nothing much had been gained. In the spring the North had been on the road to decisive victory. Farragut had broken the river defenses below New Orleans and Union troops had occupied that city, largest in the South, second commercial city in the whole country. It had seemed that nothing could stop the Union army that went crunching south after Shiloh, and the appearance had been right: nothing could have stopped it but its own commander's irresolution, overcaution, and reluctance to get in close and slug. But the whole threat had evaporated, and now it was time to make a new beginning.

The new beginning would have to be Grant's. Only from the territory he held could the right blow be launched, because the right blow would have to be aimed at Vicksburg. That city, built on high ground at a sharp bend in the Mississippi, some two hundred air miles below Memphis, had been made into a powerful fortress. Until it fell, the North could not control the river; if it fell, the Confederacy was split in two, the great traffic artery was cleared and the way was open for full conquest of the South. And while the government in Washington pondered and considered, and made ready to retire McClellan and put good-humored, fumbling Burnside in his place, and called Rosecrans out of Grant's command to take the army Buell had led so ineffectively — while all of this took shape, Grant began to plan a new offensive.

Near the end of October he sent a suggestion to Halleck. If he could get certain small reinforcements and if he might abandon some of the scattered posts he now held, he believed that he could move down the Mississippi Central Railroad — which ran from Tennessee down to Jackson, Mississippi, due east of Vicksburg — and force the

Rebels to evacuate Vicksburg. Grant spelled out the troop movements he had in mind, adding: "I am ready, however, to do with all my might whatever you may direct, without criticism."

Halleck wired his approval, and said he wanted to see an active campaign on the Mississippi that fall. Grant would be reinforced. That was fine; but Grant soon learned that more lay back of Halleck's word of approval than had been immediately visible.

John A. McClernand had sold Lincoln an idea.

As a war Democrat influential among people who detested Black Republicans, he would recruit in Illinois and neighboring states a brand-new body of troops, which he would then command in a descent on Vicksburg. Lincoln approved. Recruiting had slowed down and a terrible war weariness rested on the land. If McClernand could raise a new army corps, more power to him. Lincoln gave McClernand a letter which he might show to governors of Midwestern states, saying that when a sufficient force "not required by the operations of General Grant's command" had been raised, McClernand would be the boss of it.

For once, Halleck was in Grant's corner. He distrusted McClernand's military ability, and the thought of letting the man have an independent command in the middle of Grant's own territory horrified him; and so he proposed to make very sure that any recruits McClernand brought in would all be "required by the operations of General Grant's command." Now he wanted Grant to get moving, because some of McClernand's recruits were already en route for Memphis, and McClernand himself would be down there before long.

Grant moved promptly, but he had trouble. He went

down the railroad as he had planned, and he sent Sherman down the Mississippi with other troops, including McClernand's advance guard. The Confederates defending Vicksburg, commanded by John Pemberton, would be busy fighting Grant; while they did this, Sherman ought to be able to go in by the back door.

It might have worked, but Confederate Van Dorn slipped in behind Grant and burned his main supply base at Holly Springs, completely immobilizing him. Pemberton was able to go over to the Chickasaw Bluffs north of Vicksburg and give Sherman a bloody repulse — immediately after which an irate McClernand came down the river and, as senior, took command of Sherman and his entire expedition. Lacking anything better to do, McClernand and Sherman went over into Arkansas to pinch off a Confederate garrison at Fort Hindman, on the Arkansas River. Then they took their troops back to the big river, made camp a few miles above Vicksburg, and waited to hear from Grant.

Toward the end of January, Grant joined them there He felt that he had to: McClernand outranked everybody in the department except Grant himself, and wherever he was he would be in command unless Grant also was there. Grant did not think him fit to command — yet the man was close to Lincoln, and both Grant and the nation were indebted to him, for he had rallied the Midwestern Democracy in support of the war, he had helped to get Grant's own 21st Illinois into the service, and he had brought thousands of new soldiers into the army. His presence raised problems, but it was hard to do anything about him.

Anyway, Grant had bigger problems. Vicksburg was a

hard nut to crack. Sherman's experience showed that it could not be taken from the north, over the Chickasaw Bluffs. Obviously it could not be attacked from the west, across the river, although many expedients were being tried, including an attempt to dig a canal across the neck of land opposite Vicksburg so as to change the course of the river and leave the stronghold on dry land. As spring came on all expedients had failed. Vicksburg could be attacked only from the south and east, and all of Grant's army was on the west side of the river.

It might have been possible, of course, to go back to Memphis and start a new campaign down the railroad, along the route Grant had first chosen. But that would be to make an open confession of failure, and public sentiment in the North probably would not stand for it. The Army of the Potomac's disastrous defeat at Fredericksburg was fresh in everybody's mind, a naval thrust at Charleston was bogging down with heavy losses, there was much complaint about the seeming stalemate in front of Vicksburg . . . and anyway, Grant had always had an innate objection to retracing his steps.

So he worked out a new plan, from which grew one of the most dazzling campaigns of the war.

He would march his army south, west of the river, until he was twenty miles or more below Vicksburg. Gunboats and transports would run past the Vicksburg batteries (some of them would doubtless be sunk, but enough should get through to do what Grant wanted), and they would ferry the army across to the Mississippi side. Once across, Grant might go on down river and join forces with General Nathaniel P. Banks, who had an army in New Orleans and was under orders to co-operate with him; or he might circle around and come up to Vicksburg from the southeast or east, from which direction invading Yankees were not expected. If Pemberton marched out to meet him he might be whipped in the open field, and if not he might be penned up in Vicksburg just as Floyd and Pillow and Buckner had been penned up in Fort Donelson.

The plan was risky and Halleck probably would not like it, but Grant smoked and thought and analyzed the risks — and at last made up his mind. (By a surprising chance, of all his top generals only McClernand thought the plan was sound.) Grant would do it, no matter who did not like it. There had been enough crouching in the mud by the river. The boldest course was best. It was the one he would follow.

Deciding it that way, Grant made one of the two or three important decisions of the Civil War.

5. *Unvexed to the Sea*

THAT PART of the Mississippi still held by the Confederacy ran between two fortress towns, Vicksburg and Port Hudson, and there were a hundred and fifty miles of river between them. Those two posts were the anchors, and the looped river between them was Confederate water. Yankee gunboats now and then ran the batteries and cruised along this water, but they had no real control. As long as Vicksburg and Port Hudson held out, the Confederacy ran unbroken from the Chesapeake to the Rio Grande, and the trans-Mississippi region could send men, livestock, grain and foreign imports to the East. Also, as long as those towns held out, the Yankees could get no real use out of the rest of the river, for what the North really wanted was unbroken control clear to the Gulf.

In New Orleans was a Federal army under General Banks, former bobbin boy in a textile mill, later governor of Massachusetts and speaker of the House of Representatives, an ardent Union man with only moderate gifts as a soldier. In this spring of 1863, Banks was sending men upstream to attack Port Hudson. He was under orders to do so, anyway; the approach of his army might or might not be timed to fit with Grant's move.

At first Grant thought that it would be. He would go downstream and occupy some such east-bank town as Grand Gulf, two dozen miles south of Vicksburg. From there he would be able to send troops down to help Banks take Port Hudson. That done, his line of supply would run through New Orleans and he would have no more problems. On paper the idea looked good, and at the start it seemed to be a key part of Grant's plan.

But his success actually would not depend on any meeting with Banks. It would depend on two other things, both strictly up to Grant himself: he would have to fool the Confederates, and he would have to move very fast.

The Confederates were partly fooled already. The Federals had been very busy that winter, working on the canal project, prowling about tapping at Rebel outposts, nosing into the upriver tangle of bayous and backwaters with gunboats and transports. Pemberton was puzzled. Obviously Grant was about to do something big, but there was no way to tell where he was going to do it or what it was going to look like.

The first step came on the night of April 16, 1863, when the gunboats ran the Vicksburg batteries.

The navy was under Rear Admiral David Porter, a swaggering sea dog of the old school who began by distrusting all West Pointers and would end up by considering Grant and Sherman his blood brothers. Porter took gunboats, transports and coal barges, slipped downstream, and went pounding past the Vicksburg waterfront, while cannon boomed and exploding shell split the sky and huge bonfires on the Arkansas shore gave light for the Rebel gunners. The boats were hit repeatedly. An empty transport got a shell through the boiler and blew up with a spectacular crash, but the rest of the flotilla got through. Grant had his essential river transportation anchored below Vicksburg, ready to take his army across whenever he chose.

Next step was to move the army. Grant had three army corps here, led by McClernand, Sherman, and a handsome young engineer officer named James B. McPherson — a singularly winning character whom everybody liked, and who Sherman at least thought would eventually outclass Grant and everybody else and emerge as the great man of the war. In these three corps Grant had some forty-five thousand effectives. McClernand marched first, followed by McPherson, moving down the Louisiana side out of sight of Rebel eyes at Vicksburg. Sherman meanwhile was ostentatiously busy above Vicksburg, moving men and steamboats as if he planned to dash up the Yazoo and make another try at the Chickasaw Bluffs. His fakery was effective, and Pemberton was convinced that the big push was coming from the north. He arranged to meet it — and then, toward the end of the first week in May, he learned that he had been basely deceived and that all of Grant's army had crossed the river to the south, occupying Grand Gulf and Port Gibson and chasing out the Rebel garrisons.

So Grant was east of the river, and the campaign was well begun. At this moment Grant learned that Banks was not quite ready to move on Port Hudson. Grant would not go downstream, then; he simply could not spare the time. He would follow his original plan — cut loose from everything, destroy or scatter any Confederate field army he met, and then move in and put Vicksburg under siege.

Grant sent a message to Washington announcing his decision. Halleck would inevitably countermand it — he was the last man in the world to do as Scott had done in Mexico: cut his supply lines and gamble that he could fight his way to a decision before starvation set in. But a message to Washington had to go all the way to Cairo by steamboat before it could be put on the telegraph wires, and by the time Halleck could get an order back to Grant it would be too late.

North of Grant was Pemberton, with an army which, including fortress troops, numbered better than forty thousand men. To the east, somewhere near the state capital of Jackson, was the soldier whom Grant rated above all others in the Confederacy — Joseph E. Johnston, the winsome little strategist whose rich gifts did not include the capacity for getting along with Jefferson Davis. Grant did not know how many soldiers Johnston had, but it was certain that Johnston and Pemberton between them had more men than Grant had. The big thing was to keep them apart, beat them in detail — move fast, hit hard, and fool 'em.

So Grant left the river, and instead of marching north

for Vicksburg he went east for Jackson. He had five days' rations, carried in the men's haversacks. The Mississippi countryside would have to furnish the rest. It would also furnish wheeled transport; Grant's wagon train was a weird assemblage of carriages, buckboards and farm wagons loaded down with hams, sweet potatoes and other eatables ravished from plantation smokehouses and storerooms. Long gone were the old days when Grant sternly forbade his men to trespass on civilian property or to take civilian goods. The war was in a grimmer phase now. In the Kentucky invasion the preceding autumn, Braxton Bragg had shown how an invaded territory might be made to support an army of invasion. Earlier, Scott had shown the same thing in Mexico.

By May 15, Grant was in Jackson. Johnston had put up a fight, west of the city, but he had been driven off, and Grant had his headquarters in the Mississippi statehouse. His troops broke up railroads and destroyed factories, and then Grant wheeled about and swung west toward Vicksburg.

Pemberton was wholly confused. Johnston was ordering him to march away from Vicksburg so that the two could join forces and smash Grant, but President Davis was ordering him to hold Vicksburg at all hazards, and the luckless Pemberton was trying to do a little of both. He felt that he could pull Grant up short by cutting his supply line, and he went thrashing about manfully trying to do it — and failing utterly, because Grant had no supply line. Then Pemberton moved back to keep between Grant and Vicksburg. Grant met him at Champion's Hill and routed him, broke in his rear guard along the Black River — and on May 19. less than two weeks after he had marched away from the river, Grant had driven Pemberton into the Vicksburg lines and was digging his own line of trenches to lock him in.

He was in touch with the outside world again, for the right flank of his army rested on the Yazoo above Vicksburg and could be reached by transports and freight steamers. Joe Johnston had been driven off to the east and could not interfere, and nothing could save Vicksburg now. Just as Pemberton was getting his men back inside the Vicksburg lines, Grant got a wire from Halleck (at last!) forbidding him to do what he had just done and telling him to go South and help Banks capture Port Hudson. Grant replied that it was too late, and he settled down to the siege of Vicksburg.

Twice he tried to take the place by storm, hoping that the wearing process of a siege might not be necessary. Each assault failed, and the army settled down for the long pull. McClernand tried to cultivate the press in such a way as to get all of the credit for the coming victory; in the process he fractured army regulations so badly that Grant was able to relieve him of his command, and the war knew him no more. Reinforcements came in, and Sherman was marched east, to dig in and keep Johnston from interfering. Vicksburg was doomed, and it was only a question of time.

Even Halleck could see it now, and the War Department gave Grant everything he needed. Before long he had seventy-five thousand men in his command, and the Confederates had no chance at all to dislodge him. The army sweltered in its narrow trenches under the hot Mississippi sun, Vicksburg took a terrible daily pounding from navy guns and army mortars, Yankee engineers dug mines to blow up sections of Rebel trench, Northern and Southern boys now and then declared informal truces and met between the lines to talk things over — and in the North people looked anxiously toward Virginia, where Robert E. Lee with the dazzling Chancellorsville victory fresh on his record was marching north for a new invasion, the invisible threads of fate pulling him on toward a quiet town called Gettysburg.

Yet the real pull of fate was at Vicksburg. Lee took the eye but the pivot of the war was down here by the great river; and the final doom of the Confederacy was being written in the flaming crescent of trenches that hemmed in Pemberton's helpless army. Defeat at Gettysburg would be costly, but this blow at Vicksburg would be mortal and there would be no recovering from it. Before long the river would be open again — the coiled, tawny, eternally moving symbol of the destined unity of the nation. The road to victory led this way.

It would be easy to misunderstand the whole business, in the years to come, just as it would be easy to misunderstand the quiet little general who had brought it all to pass.

The thrust which began at Cairo and was ending at Vicksburg had never been a matter of piling up overwhelming resources and trusting that something would break under the sheer weight of men and muscle. (Halleck did try to play it that way, to be sure, on the move down to Corinth, but he had managed only to paralyze the offensive so badly that it was six months recovering.) This had been a business of finesse, of daring decisions and fast movement, of mental alertness and the ability to see and use an opening before it closed.

And the man who had and used these qualities (to the lasting benefit of the Republic) was somehow destined to go down in history as an odd combination of things that he was not.

His greatest campaign was built on speed and deception and military brilliance, but he would be written off as a man with a bludgeon, a dull plodder who could win only when he had every advantage and need count no cost. An organizer and administrator as good as the best, he would be spoken of as a man too impractical to earn his own living. He was determination and strength of will incarnate, and legend would claim him as a weakling who could not steer a straight course past the nearest bottle of whiskey. Few men of his day thought harder or straighter about the war and what it meant, but he is commonly supposed not to have thought at all, except on military matters, and then only briefly and without inspiration.

He had thought long, since the war began, about slavery itself, the dark mystery that lay at the bottom of American life like an evil stain spread across the subconscious. He had owned a slave himself once, his wife had owned several, her people had owned many, and he had not questioned the institution or voted for those who did question it. But while he was still at Cairo, with all of his campaigning ahead of him, he began to see slavery in a new light.

To his father, in the fall of 1861, he had written that he wanted to whip the Rebellion into submission, preserving all of the old institutions. And yet . . . "if it cannot be whipped in any other way than through a war against slavery, let it come to that legitimately. If it is necessary that slavery should fall that the republic may continue its existence, let slavery go."

But it was not up to the soldier to say what the war aims ought to be. Just before Shiloh he was writing to Congressman Washburne: "So long as I hold a commission in the army I have no views of my own to carry out. Whatever may be the orders of my superiors and the law, I will execute. No man can be efficient as a commander who sets his own notions above law and those whom he has sworn to obey. When Congress enacts anything too odious for me to execute, I will resign."

The creed of the regular army man could be comforting. Grant came back to it at Corinth, when he was perplexed to know how to treat civilians in occupied territory, and he put it in its simplest form: "For a soldier, his duties are plain. He is to obey the orders of all those placed over him, and whip the enemy wherever he meets him." Grimly, he added: " 'If he can' should only be thought of after an unavoidable defeat."

Yet the soldier's duty was not always clear, and literal obedience to orders might not always be enough. This war was not like the wars in which the regular's creed had been formulated, the stylized wars in which there was a great gulf fixed between the military and the civilian. This was total war, or something approaching it, and after Shiloh, Grant began to see it.

Before then it had been possible to think that after a few decisive defeats the Confederacy would simply stop fighting and sue for peace, as happened in ordinary wars. Shiloh proved that the Confederacy would not do anything of the kind. The pathetically untrained civilians who had stood in line for two days to take a hammering that the finest professional armies could hardly have endured stood for a determination that would not stop fighting as long as the physical ability to fight remained.

In which case, how did one treat enemy civilians?

Grant began to see that although one did not harm their persons one must be utterly ruthless in seizing or destroying their property, if that property might be used to support the Confederate armies. The rebellion would never be put down short of complete conquest. Capturing cities or "strategic points" would not answer. Rebel armies had to be destroyed; with them must be destroyed the ability to keep armies in existence.

Which, in turn, led back to slavery, and from deep Mississippi Grant saw that the death sentence had been written by the hard logic of wartime events.

"Slavery is already dead," he wrote, "and cannot be resurrected. It would take a standing army to maintain slavery in the South if we were to make peace today, guaranteeing to the South all their former constitutional privileges. . . . It became patent to my mind early in the rebellion that the North and South could never live at peace with each other except as one nation, and that without slavery. As anxious as I am to see peace re-established, I would not, therefore, be willing to see any settlement until this question is forever settled."

This was not quite the man who had said that as a soldier he could have no views of his own. He had views, he had hammered them out in war, and he was in a place so important, by now, that his views mattered. Nevertheless, he would always be completely subordinate. His views about the trend of the war and the goal at the end of it, which began to blend union and human freedom into a lasting amalgam, were like Lincoln's views, and that was all to the good, but Grant never forgot who was boss. When Lincoln sent an officer down the valley to recruit Negro soldiers and bespoke Grant's help for the man, Grant wrote in reply: "You may rely upon it that I will give him all the aid in my power. I would do this whether arming the Negro seemed to me a wise policy or not, because it is an order that I am bound to obey and I do not feel that in my position I have a right to question any policy of the government."

June ended, and July came; and on the third day of the month a flag of truce came across the lines, and pretty soon Grant and Pemberton were having a talk under a big tree, and the long siege was coming to an end. It would be just about this time that the great cannonade was dying away on the Pennsylvania ridges and Pickett's men were coming out to march into death and transfiguration.

Independence Day finished it. Vicksburg surrendered, thirty thousand good Confederate soldiers laid down their arms and marched off as paroled prisoners of war, and Port Hudson would follow suit as soon as the news got downstream. From President Lincoln, Grant got a letter: In his move east from the river Grant had been right and everybody in Washington (including the President himself) had been wrong, and Lincoln now wanted to make formal acknowledgment of the fact — as heart-warming a letter, perhaps, as any American soldier ever got from his President. Also from Lincoln came a more tangible reward: a commission as major general in the regular army.

The Mississippi was open now, and forever. As Lincoln told the country, "the Father of Waters again goes unvexed to the sea."

6. *The Third Star*

IT WAS HARD to get the government to see it. The capture of Vicksburg was a beginning, not an end. Occupation of the Mississippi Valley meant nothing in itself. It made possible the final conquest of the Confederacy, but it called for more aggressiveness rather than less. Victory was the moment to double the effort.

Grant wanted to strike while the enemy was still groggy. In the Vicksburg campaign the South had lost the equivalent of an army as large as that which had fought at Shiloh. Upwards of thirty-seven thousand soldiers had been captured at Port Hudson and Vicksburg; from five to ten thousand more had been killed, wounded or captured in the fighting before the siege. Always pinched for manpower, the Confederacy could not make that loss good. By no imaginable expedient could it prevent the victorious Federal army, in July of 1863, from smashing deep into the heart of the Southland, destroying food supplies and munitions factories, closing ports and bringing final conquest within reach.

Aside from its troops in the trans-Mississippi department, the Confederacy now had only one sizable army west of the Alleghenies: Braxton Bragg's, in central Tennessee, against which Rosecrans was beginning to maneuver with the army which had been Buell's. Grant proposed to march straight down to Mobile, on the Gulf, establish a supply base there, and then go fanning out northward with fire and sword, cutting Bragg's rear out from under him. Twice in July and once early in August he asked

Washington to sanction such a move. But Halleck had other ideas.

To begin with, Halleck was not satisfied with Grant's action in releasing the Vicksburg prisoners on parole. They should have been shipped to Northern prison camps, he said, to be returned to the South only when properly exchanged for Federal prisoners. Grant simply replied that most of Pemberton's men lived in the South-west; freed on parole, they were likely to go home and stay there, out of the war for keeps. Also, to ship thirty thousand men up the river to Cairo and then overland to Maryland — the depot for prisoners awaiting exchange — would have been fearfully expensive. The onetime quartermaster was a careful man with a government dollar.

But this was minor. What mattered was that Halleck disapproved of further offensives. The victorious army must be split up, a garrison here and a garrison there, some men sent to Banks in New Orleans and others back to Kentucky, with still more going off to Missouri and others detached to hold different points in Mississippi. By midsummer the concentration of troops that had taken Vicksburg had been dissolved. The offensive Grant had in mind was no longer possible.

It was a pity, because Rosecrans had begun to press Bragg with considerable skill. Rosecrans had been in and around Murfreesboro, Tennessee, ever since the first of the year. His army had fought a desperate, inconclusive battle with Bragg's just as 1862 came to a close, and it had been six months recovering. During most of the Vicksburg campaign Rosecrans had been immobile, although Grant had been pleading for action, but toward the end of June he came to life and took his army of fifty thousand men out on the offensive.

With a slightly smaller force Bragg held strong positions in the uplands west of the Cumberland plateau, defensive points which he had been fortifying for months and which were very formidable. Rosecrans had no intention of attacking them head on. By a series of fast, cleverly concealed marches he maneuvered Bragg out of them and forced him to retreat behind the Tennessee River. Pressing his advantage, he forced Bragg clear out of the state and into northern Georgia, and the highly important city of Chattanooga fell into his hands without a struggle.

As everyone could easily see afterward, with the advantage of hindsight, Rosecrans ought to have moved into Chattanooga, consolidated his army, and gone on from there only after a careful regrouping of his forces. But Bragg seemed to be in headlong flight and Rosecrans was bubbling with confidence. He pressed on in pursuit, incautiously letting the several corps of his army get widely separated — and in mid-September Bragg turned and struck.

If he had turned just a little more quickly and struck a trifle more sharply Bragg might have given the North its worst setback of the war, for Rosecrans was not ready for battle. Bragg's turnabout was just slow enough and his swing to the offensive was just hesitant enough to give the Federals warning, and Rosecrans pulled his army together behind Chickamauga Creek, just south of the Tennessee–Georgia line and a dozen miles from Chattanooga.

It was well that he had been given a few days' grace, for when the Confederates hit him they hit hard. The Davis government had been profoundly alarmed by the prospect of an invasion of its heartland — Grant had correctly judged that the march of a Union army south of Tennessee and east of Mississippi was something which the Confederacy could not at any cost permit — and it had taken the unheard-of step of weakening Lee's army in order to help Bragg, sending the redoubtable James Longstreet and his equally redoubtable corps of infantry down to lend a hand. These reached Bragg on the eve of battle, and in a tremendous two-day engagement Rosecrans's army was crumpled up, driven in wild retreat, and all but destroyed. Only a heroic stand by troops under George Thomas kept the Federal disaster from being absolute.

Back in Chattanooga the beaten Union army took uneasy refuge. Bragg's victorious troops held the high ground overlooking the city, Missionary Ridge and Lookout Mountain, and blocked the only convenient avenue by which Rosecrans could get supplies. It seemed very likely that Rosecrans would soon have to surrender or to beat a retreat which — since almost impassable mountain roads were all that were open to him — would cause his army to fall apart and die. To make matters still worse, General Burnside had taken a smaller Union army into eastern Tennessee to occupy Knoxville, just far enough away so that he could not help Rosecrans but near enough so that if Rosecrans sank he would inevitably go down too.

By the final week in September the picture in the West had completely changed. Just as Bragg's invasion of Kentucky in 1862 had threatened to undo everything won at Donelson and Shiloh, so now his victory at Chickamauga threatened to cancel the gains made at Vicksburg. For the second time, Halleck's passion for dispersion and a cautious defensive had given the Confederates an opening. It was very fortunate for the North that Bragg was never able to take full advantage of it.

Grant had gone down to New Orleans to consult with General Banks. Banks gave a grand review for him, and in tribute to Grant's fame as a horseman presented him with a spirited horse, not yet broken to the saddle. Grant rode the beast, it shied at a passing steam engine and ran away, and Grant was thrown to the ground. The fall knocked him unconscious and left him painfully crippled for weeks. (It was whispered, of course, that he was drunk. Whenever anything happened to Grant someone was sure to wink and wag the head and drop hints about the bottle.)

While he was recovering frantic telegrams came from Washington: Send help to Rosecrans, send every man he could spare, send somebody competent in command. (He sent Sherman and McPherson.) While the troops were moving Grant himself was ordered north for a conference. Still lame, able to ride a horse only if someone helped him into the saddle, Grant went up the river, and eventually he clambered aboard a train at Indianapolis and met the Secretary of War, Edwin M. Stanton.

They did not get off to a good start. Grant's staff was with him, and the bustling cabinet member walked up to a staff surgeon, a blameless physician who wore full whiskers under a campaign hat, pumped his hand, and cried authoritatively: "How do you do, General Grant! I recognized you from your pictures!" That was straightened out, of course — although Grant and Stanton never did really warm up to each other — and Grant got his orders.

Unified command in the West was restored, and Grant now was in charge of everything between the Alleghenies and the Mississippi. He was to go to Chattanooga at once, and he could either retain Rosecrans in command there or replace him with Thomas. Without hesitation Grant chose Thomas, and in a short time he himself was on his way south. By the latter part of October he was in Chattanooga.

Strong reinforcements came in; a good part of Grant's own Army of the Tennessee, and two army corps from the Army of the Potomac under Joe Hooker. General Thomas, who was certainly one of the four or five best soldiers on either side in the whole war, restored the confidence of Rosecrans's old army, the Army of the Cumberland. Plans to reopen the supply line and break Bragg's grip on the place had been worked out, and it is quite possible that the Federals would ultimately have beaten the encircling Rebels and regained the initiative even if Grant had never gone near Chattanooga.

But he did go there and on his arrival things began to happen. The old atmosphere of a doomed army waiting for catastrophe vanished; now there was a sense that someone who knew how to make war was organizing victory. The Confederate squeeze on the supply route was broken and full rations were restored. Grant might not have done it all but it began with him, and soldiers who had had a hard time of it found confidence in the very sight of him.

Not until November 23 was Grant ready to fight. The battle lasted three days, it ended in overwhelming victory — and it did not go at all as Grant had planned.

Grant planned to have Thomas's Army of the Cumberland make a holding attack on Bragg's lofty position along Missionary Ridge. Hooker, meanwhile, would knock Bragg's left loose from the slopes of Lookout Mountain.

and Sherman with the Army of the Tennessee would cross the river above Chattanooga, get astride the upper end of Missionary Ridge, and crumple up the Confederate right.

Hooker did his part, Thomas threatened the center — but Sherman could not carry out his assignment, chiefly because the Union chiefs had misunderstood the topography. It was no continuous ridge which he faced, but a chain of hills. There was nothing for him to get astride of; instead he had to fight his way from hill to hill, and the Confederates fought with terrible tenacity and gave him a decisive and costly check.

Thomas moved his men forward, to press the Confederate center and take the pressure off Sherman . . . and the men of the Army of the Cumberland, suffering a slow burn because the lesser role which had been given them clearly implied that the commanding general had little confidence in them, suddenly took things into their own hands and went swarming straight up the steep slope of Missionary Ridge without orders. Clear over the crest they went in a fantastic, almost unbelievable charge that broke the Confederate army in half and sent the fragments pelting back into Georgia.

When he saw the battle lines start up that slope Grant angrily demanded who had ordered such a suicidal charge — the men would be butchered, the attack could not possibly succeed; whoever was responsible was going to sweat for it. One of the first generals to get to the top of the ridge shouted to the cheering, capering soldiers, "You'll all be court-martialed!" — and then broke out in a great shout of laughter.

No one was any more amazed than Bragg himself. He fumed and swore, declaring that the position was so strong a mere skirmish line ought to have held it. Actually, the place was weaker than it looked. The assault waves got a good deal of protection from gullies and hollows in the mountain slope, and defenders firing down from such a height usually shot too high. Oddly enough, the Union soldiers themselves tended to give Grant all of the credit. "All we needed was a leader," they explained.

However the soldiers might feel, the country at large believed that the miraculous business was all Grant's doing. The tragedy of Chickamauga had been avenged, Burnside's column was safe again, once more the door to the heart of the South was open. The general who had capped Vicksburg with Chattanooga was obviously a master soldier, and after Chattanooga it was inevitable that all of the war would be turned over to him.

There was a rough justice at work here. The long campaign that won Vicksburg and broke the Confederacy's back had been overshadowed by the more spectacular war in the East, and Gettysburg, whose importance was wholly negative, was taken for the decisive battle of the year. If Grant got more credit than was strictly his due for Chattanooga it only made up for the earned credit that had not been given him earlier. The decision to promote him to the top spot was right, no matter how it had been reached.

As winter came, Congress revived the old rank of lieutenant general. Grant was nominated for the job, the nomination was quickly confirmed, and in March, 1864, he was called to Washington and given supreme command of the country's armies. (Did some fugitive memory from the dim past, one wonders, recall the moment on the West Point parade ground when the cadet from Illinois looked at Winfield Scott and briefly dared picture himself as the panoplied general of the armies? Probably not. Grant seems never to have bothered to strut for the benefit of his inner eye.) By springtime Grant was in Virginia, planning the climactic campaigns of the war.

His hands were not entirely free. Banks was being sent on an expedition up the Red River into (it was hoped) Texas, for reasons which neatly blended high policy and low politics. The French were in Mexico, and it would be well to overawe them; also, much cotton could doubtless be scooped up. Grant objected to this campaign. It pointed in the wrong direction and it would use troops needed elsewhere. But he was overruled and he had to make the best of it.

It did not matter too much. He was free at last to do what he had always wanted to do — strike through the deep South, cutting the Confederacy into successively smaller pieces and destroying (as we would say now) the war potential which kept its armies in the field. There would be no more dispersion of strength to hold isolated places. The national force must concentrate and it must move, always closing in and giving the weaker side no respite; the rising power of the Federal government must be applied remorselessly until no one could believe that there might be two nations between Mexico and Canada.

To do all of this Grant had to smash two Confederate armies. (There were other troops in gray, to be sure — beyond the Mississippi, in coastal fortifications, and in various local detachments — but only these two really mattered.) One was the fabulous Army of Northern Virginia, lean and muscular, led by Robert E. Lee; the other was the Army of Tennessee, the hard-luck organization that Bragg had never quite been able to handle, commanded now by Joseph E. Johnston. While these armies existed, Jefferson Davis's government lived. When they died, it would die.

Grant undoubtedly would have preferred to stay in the South and move with the armies that marched against Johnston and the untouched Southern hinterland. He soon saw that he could not do that. Left to itself, the Union Army of the Potomac could not pin down the Confederate Army of Northern Virginia and take it out of the war. It was a good army, but it had a tradition of defeat. Cliques and jealousies ran through its officer corps. Its commanders had lived too long under the shadow of Lee. Over and over this army had taken the offensive, and each time Lee had seized the initiative, forced it to move in step with his moves, and finally driven it back in bloody, humiliating defeat.

The fault did not particularly lie with George G. Meade, the grizzled, devoted, ill-tempered soldier who commanded the Army of the Potomac. The fault was in the terrible past, in the fate that made the defense of Washington a crippling responsibility beneath every attempted offensive, in the paralyzing hand of caution which the War Department always kept upon this army. With supreme courage the Army of the Potomac had fought for three years — but when Grant went down into Virginia to have a look at it, he found it camped within twenty-five miles of the site of the first battle it ever fought, Bull Run. To gain those twenty-five miles the army to date had suffered just under one hundred and forty thousand casualties.

Grant must go with the Army of the Potomac. He knew very well that the war would not be won in Virginia. The road to victory, now as always, lay far to the South. But if the North could not win the war in Virginia it could easily lose it there. Balanced against the declining Southern will to resist was the Northern will to conquer. Northern men when they looked at the war saw Virginia first of all — Virginia, and the dreadful list of Northern boys killed and wounded there. One more great disaster in Virginia might make the Northern will flicker and go out, just as an earlier disaster in Virginia had at last extinguished the British will and had permitted a new nation to come to birth. Sherman and Thomas and McPherson could follow the road to victory. The general in chief must stay at the danger point.

It was so arranged. March and April wore away, while a great frenzy of preparation possessed the North — men and hardtack, cannon and mules, miles of wagons and prodigious warehouses, every ounce of power the land could produce, carefully marshaled for the supreme moment of trial. On May 4, 1864, everything was ready and all of the armies began to move — in northern Georgia, in the Shenandoah Valley, up the James River, south across the historic fords of the Rapidan. Grant rode with the Army of the Potomac, a stooped figure in a worn uniform, three stars on his bent shoulders, an indomitable resolve in his heart.

7. *The Qualities of Grandeur*

THE FINAL YEAR was smoke and dust and bloodshed and death, the ending and beginning of dreams, and the creation of undying legend out of mist and flame. The armies moved in for their last grapple, and there would be no stop to their fighting until one side or the other could fight no more.

As the armies moved, the chance of war made certain homely American place names terrible — Spotsylvania Courthouse and Kenesaw Mountain, Cold Harbor and Peachtree Creek, Brice's Cross Roads and Ezra Church and Yellow Tavern and Cedar Creek, and that epic of fire and agony which is remembered, simply, as the Wilderness. Each of these, and many more besides, killed and maimed its thousands, and seemed at the moment to stand by itself, unique and dreadful, a frightening symbol of men's capacity for going deep into the hidden kingdom of violence. . . . In the end, these battles add up to an amazing and pathetic gamble by men of the North and men of the South that somehow, in the long run, the whole business would prove worth what it had cost.

Those battles of 1864 can be read about separately. An extensive literature built around them contains some of the most dramatic chapters in the whole story of the Civil War. Yet in essence the final year of the war was one prolonged, unified battle in which the individual struggles were hardly more than incidents. With single command had come a single plan. The war was no longer a succession of great feats of arms performed to the applause of soldiers, governments and the outside world. It was now a grim business of applying all the pressure possible and waiting for something to break.

It was a chancy business, to be sure, for no one could be certain what would break first. On paper it was clear enough: the North could apply more pressure than the South could stand. But it cost the ordinary folk of the

North just as much, emotionally, to turn the screw as it cost the ordinary folk of the South to endure the turning. If both sides were fighting for abstractions, the Northern abstraction was just a little further removed from the realities of daily living than the Southern abstraction, and hence was apt to grow indistinct a little sooner. The North could lose the war in this final year, not through outright defeat but through loss of willingness to pay the price of victory. Grant had taken hold of the war and victory would be had if the price were paid, but the price was likely to be high.

Grant was part of a unique team. He was a realist, seeing clearly how the country could get what the country professed to want. The other half of the team was Abraham Lincoln, who knew — perhaps better than any other American has ever known — how to appraise the temper of his fellow countrymen and how to put into that temper, subtly and mysteriously, an occasional trace of his own high resolve. He underwrote Grant's program. In effect, he pledged that Northern endurance would be ample for the job at hand. In the end it developed that he knew what he was talking about. Because he was right, Grant also was right.

As far as the Virginia campaign went, Grant's moment of decision came very quickly.

The Army of the Potomac moved down into the tangled Wilderness region below the Rapidan, trying to slip past Lee's right flank and force him to fight in the open country. Lee sent his troops in fast and hard to strike the Federals in the Wilderness, where advantages in numbers and in artillery would tend to disappear. Grant and Meade met the attack with a counterblow of their own, and a fantastic battle boiled and eddied for two days in a dark forest where generals could see neither their own men nor the enemy. In its entire career the Army of the Potomac had had no worse fighting. It lost more than seventeen thousand men, some of them burned to death in a forest fire that complicated the fighting — and to all seeming it had had a defeat as disastrous as that of Chancellorsville, fought almost exactly one year earlier on almost exactly the same ground.

By tradition and by past performance, the army would now recross the Rapidan, nurse its wounds, call for reinforcements and more equipment, and after a month or so set out to make war anew — probably to counter some move of Lee's, who would take advantage of the lull to start an offensive of his own.

Grant held his army in its lines one day — and then marched south, for all the world as if the battle had been won and not lost.

When the move began the soldiers supposed that they were retreating, as they had done so many times before. When they came to a crossroad and, in the gloom of a smoke-stained night, found that they were taking the turn that would plunge them more deeply into enemy territory, they set up a sudden cheer. Whatever else Grant might mean, he meant no turning back. The days of retreat were over.

The soldiers now were on the road to the most sustained fighting of the war. For more than a month there was not a day in which some parts of the two armies were not in close contact. At places like Spotsylvania Courthouse and Cold Harbor there were long-drawn battles as deadly as anything in military history. In between there were slogging marches down hot dusty roads, with cavalry patrols and infantry skirmishers thrusting at each other. And always there was fighting, of greater or lesser intensity, and Federal losses for the month averaged close to two thousand men a day.

Each battle looked very much like a Federal defeat — except that afterward the Army of the Potomac always moved on toward the south, quite as if it had won; and at last there had been set in motion a tide that would sweep the Confederacy out of existence no matter what skill or valor tried to stay it.

Skill and valor of breath-taking quality were indeed displayed in the Confederate defense. The Army of the Potomac was never quite able to get in between its foe and the Confederate capital, so as to force a finish fight in the open. Lee always kept one step ahead, and the Northerners were forever compelled to attack, with heavy losses. Yet in the long run Lee could do no more than stave off defeat. He could never seize the initiative, as he had always done before. He was compelled to fight the kind of war he could not win. Sooner or later he would be in the lines around Richmond, forced to stand a siege, and a siege could end in only one way.

Because the North mustered more men than the South it could better stand battle casualties — on paper, at any rate — and so the Virginia campaign of 1864 is often written down as a mere war of attrition, with the Federal commander callously trading two lives for one in order to wear out his opponent. Actually, Grant was playing a far different game. He was winning the war, as he had always planned, in the deep South. What was important about the Virginia campaign was that it kept Lee pinned down and helpless, unable to detach troops or create a diversion to relieve Joe Johnston in his hopeless task of defending the Confederacy's vitals.

Johnston did as well as anyone could have done. Against Sherman's advance he sparred and sideslipped and hit back when he could, and Sherman played him cautiously. Indeed — as Johnston acidly pointed out, when Davis finally replaced him with the headlong fighter John B. Hood — it had actually taken Sherman longer to drive him into the entrenchments around Atlanta than it had taken Grant to drive Lee into the fortifications about Petersburg and Richmond. But the assignment was impossible. Atlanta fell, and after a series of rather pointless maneuvers across northern Georgia, Sherman left Thomas to guard Tennessee and struck out for the seacoast.

Hood ignored him, went north on a doomed counter-invasion, half wrecked his army in a desperate offensive at Franklin, Tennessee, and came to total disaster at Nashville, where Thomas almost destroyed him, routing him in a wild two-day battle that took Hood's army out of the war for keeps. Sherman came to the surface at Savannah before the end of the year; the Confederacy now consisted of no more than southern Virginia and the Carolinas, and there was no chance at all to keep Sherman from marching up the coast and ending it. The victorious drive had started at Fort Donelson, and at Vicksburg the door had been broken open, and now the inevitable clincher was being applied.

Grant's Virginia campaign, in other words, makes sense only when viewed as part of the total picture — for which, it must be remembered, Grant bore the responsibility.

That hard advance from the Rapidan to the James,

made at such frightful cost, and those dreary weeks in the Petersburg trenches that had seemed to be sheer useless waste and tragedy — these had been essential in the grand strategy of the last year of the war. They had compelled the Richmond government to keep facing north while Sherman and Thomas took the Confederacy to pieces behind its back. Thousands of soldiers in the Army of the Potomac died before Sherman ever reached Atlanta or made his fabulous, all-destroying march to the sea, but they had made his conquests possible. In the end, as Sherman moved grimly on to the consummation of his design, Davis could do no better than go to Georgia and make speeches to oppose him.

Few of Grant's subordinates served him as well as did Sherman and Thomas. Banks ran into trouble with his Red River expedition and hurried back to New Orleans in disgrace, having done no more than keep thousands of good Union soldiers from pulling their weight that final summer. Ben Butler failed utterly, trying to come up the south bank of the James River while Grant and Meade marched down from the Rapidan, and the blow that might have taken Richmond and ended the war ahead of time became a dismal fiasco. Generals Franz Sigel and David Hunter failed, in succession, to close the Confederacy's great granary and strategic highway in the Shenandoah Valley, and their failure added months to the fighting required of the Army of the Potomac.

Unfortunately, for a while those failures were all that people could see. They came just when the terrible casualty lists from Virginia were at their worst, and the combination strained Northern endurance to the uttermost. In midsummer Lincoln himself believed that he would not be re-elected, and like nearly everyone else he assumed that a lost election would mean a lost war. But just when things looked worst, Sherman captured Atlanta, and bluff old Admiral Farragut damned the torpedoes and broke his way into Mobile Bay, and Phil Sheridan burned out the beautiful and dangerous garden spot of the Shenandoah, destroying the Confederate army that had defended the place — and, in the end, it was Southern endurance that broke.

Desertion began to cripple Southern armies, as men who were convinced that their cause could not win slipped away and went home, to try to salvage for themselves and their families whatever might be saved from the general destruction. Disaffection born of foreknowledge of disaster crippled the Confederate government, and the Confederate Congress wildly debated whether to give freedom to Negro slaves in order to make soldiers of them — debating it with just as much heat as if freedom for all slaves were not riding down the wind with the tramp of approaching Yankee armies — and when it was time to halt Sherman on his march across the Carolinas the government could assemble an imposing array of generals but hardly any private soldiers.

The house was coming down, and after four stormy years of life the Southern Confederacy, with all the dreams that possessed it, was entering the darkness of blown-out stars and echoing night, leaving the unbroken fabric of the American Union dyed with an ineradicable streak of passion and remembered glory.

The break came at the end of March, 1865. Sherman was far up in North Carolina now, watched again by Joe Johnston, who had been restored too late to command of an army which, as Johnston himself confessed, could do no more than annoy its antagonist. Far in the South a great army of Union cavalry armed with repeating rifles and led by young General James H. Wilson was slicing across Alabama, destroying the last of the South's war industries there, too powerful for even Bedford Forrest to drive away.

In the lines before Petersburg, Lee made a last despairing effort to break the Union grip and failed, and then Sheridan took cavalry and infantry in on Lee's extreme right, smashed the force that was sent out to stop him, and cut the railroad that linked Petersburg to what was left of the South. Meade struck Lee's thinned trench line with the 6th Army Corps and made the break-through the Federals had been hoping for so long — and by April 3 the Army of Northern Virginia had abandoned Richmond and Petersburg and was in full flight, hoping against hope that it might reach Johnston's forces and somehow, somewhere, whip either Sherman or Grant or perhaps both of them together and so keep the war going a little longer.

It was hope born of delirium. Grant moved out in pursuit, as swift and as sure in movement now as in the Vicksburg campaign. He swung around in front and drove Lee west instead of letting him go south, closing all avenues of escape, striking the fugitive army as it moved and cutting down what was left of its fighting power. And the pleasant little courthouse town of Appomattox moved into American legend forever when Lee at last was at bay there, overpowering enemies on all sides, no food left for his men, half of the soldiers that remained too weak and dispirited to carry weapons or to form line as organized troops.

It was Palm Sunday, and Lee rode to the house of a man named McLean to have a talk with Grant. He wore his best uniform and he had a sword buckled at his side, and there should have been lancers and pennons and trumpets going on before, for he was the last American knight and he had a grandeur about him, and when he rode out of the war something that will never come back rode out of American life with him.

Great moments provide their own dramatic contrast. Grant came to the meeting in the coat of a private soldier, with tarnished shoulder straps tacked on, and his boots and uniform were spattered with mud. He had forgotten to wear his sword — as an eminently practical man he hardly ever bothered with it; during the great battle of the Wilderness his side arm had been a jackknife, with which he pensively whittled twigs while the fighting raged — and there was nothing at all imposing about him as he sat down, for the third time in this war, to write the terms of surrender for an opposing army. The beaten man looked the part of a great soldier; the victor looked perhaps like a clerk from a Galena leather store, unaccountably rigged out in faded regimentals, scribbling on a scratch pad in the front room of a little house in southern Virginia.

The terms were simple. The beaten army would not go off to prison camp, any more than had been the case after Vicksburg. The men would lay down their weapons and then they would go home; and since most of them were small farmers, and the war was about over, Grant directed that each one who claimed to own a horse or a mule be allowed to take one home with him from the stock of captured Confederate army animals. The men would need these beasts to get in a crop and work their farms, said Grant. No one knew better than he the heartbreak of trying to get a living from the land with inadequate equipment.

And he wrote into the terms of surrender one of the great sentences in American history. Officers and men were to sign paroles, and then they were to go home, "not to be disturbed by the United States authority so long as they observe their paroles and the laws in force where they reside."

Grant looked at the beaten army and he saw his own fellow Americans, who had made their fight and lost and now wanted to go back and rebuild. But the war had aroused much hatred and bitterness, especially among those who had done no fighting, and Grant knew very well that powerful men in Washington were talking angrily of treason and of traitors, and wanting to draw up proscription lists, so that leading Confederates could be jailed or hanged.

The sentence Grant had written would make that impossible. They could proceed against Robert E. Lee, for instance, only by violating the pledged word of U. S. Grant, who had both the will and the power to see his word kept inviolate. If they could not hang Lee they could hardly hang anybody. There would be no hangings. Grant had ruled them out.

It did not strike the eye quite as quickly, but U. S. Grant had a certain grandeur about him, too.

I I I

The General in Politics

1. *Roads Leading Down*

I T HAD BEEN a dazzling rise. Ten years earlier he had been a discredited ex-captain of infantry, a man who could not make a go of it in the regular army at a time when the regulars were supposed to offer a final haven for the shiftless and the irresponsible. In civilian life he had been a misfit, living under a pattern of ill luck so consistent that somehow it seemed that he himself must be mostly responsible for it.

Now, in the spring of 1865, Ulysses S. Grant was at the peak. Every reality of the old days had been inverted. The military life which he had always disliked had turned out to be the calling made for him. The army which, in the person of a grumpy post commander, had considered him unfit was under his sole command; with it he had won the greatest war in his country's history. Indecision had been replaced by sharp decisiveness, drifting by direct action, ineffectiveness by a smooth and effortless competence. If he wanted reward, his fellow countrymen were prepared to give him anything they could; if he wanted to continue in their service they were likely to put the heaviest of all responsibilities on his shoulders.

Even in America, where the rags-to-riches, log-cabin-to-the-White-House story was the cornerstone of national folklore, there had never been anything quite like this.

Yet in the very perfection of his triumph there existed the beginning of tragedy. The one job for which he was supremely fitted had been given to him and he had finished it. His overwhelming success meant that other jobs would be given to him, and they would be radically different. They would, in fact, demand qualities quite the opposite of the ones that had brought him to his present high place. At the crest, any road he took would lead downward.

He would walk that road with his country, because in good fortune and in bad, in his strengths and in his weaknesses, he was the perfect representative of the land that bore him. His story is a strange allegory of America itself, of the way failure follows success, of the incomprehensible manner in which the endowment that wins a noble victory is never the endowment that can use the victory after it has been won. There is a will-o'-the-wisp strain flickering through American history, an unending effort to lay hands on a great prize clearly seen, fairly won and then strangely elusive.

Surprisingly enough, the nation most resembled Grant in its underlying relationship to the military arts and war.

Like Grant, it did not care very much for soldiering, and in ordinary times it felt ill at ease about it. It contributed little to military theory, simply because it never put its best brains to work thinking about it. Weapons of course were pure gadgets, invented or elaborated with great ingenuity, but war was a very different question, ap-

parently quite a dull one, and it got no particular attention. The country never went to war properly prepared
for it.

Yet when war did come the nation seemed to find itself.
It showed an amazing competence in the practice of those
military arts which it professed to despise. After a certain
amount of preliminary fumbling, it discovered that making war consisted chiefly in summoning up all of the energy, force and resources possible and in applying them
inflexibly and with a single eye to the accomplishment of
a desired task — in wartime, the task of making the enemy
surrender.

It was precisely in that sort of activity that the genius of
the country lay. For generations it had had more energy
and force and resources than it knew what to do with; its
chief interest was always in finding the most effective ways
to use them. War provided a different sort of goal, chal-
lenging the country to take its predominant talent and use
it to the very fullest degree.

As a result, a nation which did not especially like to
think about war and which had very little use for military
tradition and ritual turned out to be amazingly warlike
when the test came. It detested war, but when the time
came for thinking with the muscles and the viscera, war
fitted as a glove fits the hand. It required the American
to do with all of his might that which he did best anyway, and at the same moment it relieved him of the need
to do any serious thinking about what was likely to come
of it all.

When the war called on Grant and others in the North
to be soldiers, it was simply demanding that they be themselves. They responded, and in the process they became

soldiers of a kind not often met in the military textbooks. So they won an enormous victory.

And then, having won it, they did not know what to do with it.

. . . the will-o'-the-wisp again, recurrent in American history. Victory becomes an end in itself, and "unconditional surrender" expresses all anyone wants to look for, because if the enemy gives up unconditionally he is completely and totally beaten and all of the complex problems which made an enemy out of him in the first place will probably go away and nobody will have to bother with them any more. The golden age is always going to return just as soon as the guns have cooled and the flags have been furled, and the world's great age will begin anew the moment the victorious armies have been demobilized. Victory is to be a business of getting back to an ideal condition that existed before a regrettable quarrel somehow got out of hand.

When it fails to work out that way there is always a big letdown. Then the political leaders are blamed, because they are obliged to call for readjustments to a reality which falls a great deal short of the contemplated ideal. Such readjustments nobody likes, and it becomes easy to feel that perhaps the soldier's way is better — the cutting of a direct path through comprehended obstacles to a perfectly tangible goal.

And after a while, if the soldier who led in the cutting of that path is an unassuming and likable man (flamboyance will always be suspect) and has an obvious and uncomplicated integrity, he is apt to find himself in a wholly new role, called on for something very like the working of miracles . . . miracles, because what is really

expected of him is that he will take the insoluble problems on himself and bring back the good old days when
life was fairer and simpler.

General Grant after Appomattox is the classic example.

The war had been won and yet the golden age ob-
stinately refused to return. The Union had been restored,
but an enormous amount of work obviously had to be
done before it would again be the mystic thing men had
died for. Slavery had been abolished, but the Negro free
presented as many problems as the Negro enslaved — different problems, to be sure, but numerous and perplexing.

The war in short had been a point of departure rather
than a terminus. Instead of reaching a quiet harbor where
the anchor could be dropped, the sails furled and the crew
sent ashore, the vessel had gone beyond the headlands and
far out on the open sea, and there would be no turning
back. Nothing was ever going to be the same again, a dull
awareness of the fact was stirring — and here was the man
who had won the war, the man who said little but did
much, the magnanimous man who did not hate his enemies and who therefore must understand peace as well
as war.

Nothing could have been more natural than for the
country to suppose that he was the man who could best
lead it through the bewildering complexities of the postwar years. And for Grant nothing could have been more
unfortunate, because such a role called on him to trans-
cend the national character; and instead of transcending
it he embodied it.

Unfortunate for the country, too, beyond doubt; yet less
so, for Grant was symbol rather than cause of the darkness
that came down after the war ended.

And that darkness was never absolute. Two ideas had been broadened and made enduring by the war, if for no better reason than that a great many men had died for them, or were thought to have done so: the idea of human unity and the idea of human freedom. Henceforth these ideas would belong to all Americans and there would be no getting away from them. Even as it had been making democracy ever so much more difficult to operate, the war had been committing the country to it forever, and in the years of the nation's grossest materialism its noblest ideals would be taking root.

Grant's bitter fortune was that he came to symbolize the materialism. Yet it was the ideals that he really understood, and he had done his full share to give them life.

2. *The Word of General Grant*

DESTINY HAS A WAY of working while people look the other way. A man will make a snap judgment on some matter of no importance whatever — he will decide, for instance, whether or not he will go to the theater with friends on a certain evening — and this decision, which seems to concern nothing more than the way a few leisure hours are to be spent, will affect all the rest of his life, and the course of a nation's history as well.

On Good Friday in 1865 — April 14 by the calendar — U. S. Grant had such a decision to make.

President and Mrs. Lincoln were to go to Ford's Theater to see a popular actress in a so-so play. The President did not particularly want to go, but there was a holiday mood on the town, the theater management had announced that he would be present, and he felt that he could hardly get out of it. Would General and Mrs. Grant care to go along?

Grant liked the theater well enough, but on this evening, less than a week after Lee's surrender, he and Mrs. Grant were anxious to get to Burlington, New Jersey, where their older children were in school. Also, it appears that when the Lincolns visited army headquarters at City Point that spring, Mrs. Lincoln had been nervous, irritable, and in truth quite hard to get along with, and Mrs. Grant did not especially want any more of her company just then. So Grant made his excuses, and that evening he and Mrs. Grant took the train; and before he went to bed that night Grant learned that he (or, more accurately, Mrs. Grant) had made one of the most momentous decisions of his life.

For John Wilkes Booth was also of the party at Ford's Theater that evening, and he carried out the monstrous, scatterbrained plan which had taken him there. If Grant had been in the box with the President he almost certainly would have been murdered. Booth had included him in his program for the evening. . . .

There is a tale of a mysterious horseman, riding up in the dusk to peer into the carriage that was taking Mrs. Grant and her youngest son, Jesse, to the railroad station — a horseman who rode off furiously when he saw that Grant was not there. (Grant had been delayed and took another cab, meeting his family at the station.) There is also a tale of a man who tried to force his way into the Grants' car on the train, who wrestled with the brakeman on the open platform and was at last thrown from the moving train, and who long afterward wrote an unsigned letter to Mrs. Grant saying that he was glad he had not been able to do what he had been supposed to do on Good Friday night.

All in all, because he went to New Jersey instead of to the theater, Grant got twenty more years of life, became President of the United States, knew the pinnacle of fame, and bewilderment and disillusion as well, left his great name to one of the shabbiest eras in American history, and missed the apotheosis that bore Lincoln aloft as in a chariot of fire once Booth's derringer had done its work.

Grant did go to New Jersey, and by any ordinary standard it would seem that his luck had been in, that night when he inadvertently steered clear of the man who wanted to kill him. Yet after Lincoln was gone nothing, finally, went quite right for Grant.

He learned about Lincoln's assassination when his train got to Philadelphia, and he hurried back to Washington, reflecting gloomily that the President's death had set back the reconstruction of the nation incalculably. He knew what Lincoln wanted, because he and the President had done much talking about it during the final month of the war, and they had been in full agreement. The country was reunited and slavery was dead, and they felt that men of good will must go on to rebuild as rapidly as they could, wasting no time or energy on reprisals and hatred, treating the men of the South as friends and not as enemies.

The new President had a very different viewpoint.

The new President was Andrew Johnson, of whom

Grant had seen rather more than he wanted down in Tennessee during the war. Johnson was a hard, blunt, unterrified and wholly determined man, who had come up from the very bottom of the heap, the son of a Southern poor white, a former tailor's apprentice, a self-made man who had had no schooling and no advantages. He was sensitive about his plebeian origin, and to cover his sensitivity he boasted about it, thrusting his lowly birth into people's faces with bristling pugnacity. He had had a famous passage at arms with Jefferson Davis, in Congress, years before the war; thinking that Davis was patronizing him, he had lashed out bitterly at "the illegitimate, swaggering, bastard, scrub aristocracy" of the cotton South. This spring, inaugurated Vice-President of the United States, he had made a confused, rambling, bombastic inaugural address in the Senate chamber, ranting about his own rise from the bottom of society, leaving most of his embarrassed hearers believing that he was drunk.

A Tennessean, he had been stout for the Union and had served as war governor in that battle-torn state at a time when it took courage to speak and act for the Union there. This spring, as the Confederacy crumbled to dust, Johnson had spoken out of the depths of his bitterness: Southern leaders were criminals and should be hanged, "treason must be made odious," traitors must be impoverished and punished. He had been so very bitter that even vengeful Republican radicals like Ben Wade and Zachariah Chandler, who were quite willing to see all of Dixie treated as a conquered province, felt uneasily that he might be a little too rigorous about it all.

Now he was President, and Jefferson Davis was a prisoner. If any forbearance was shown the South it would have to come from Andy Johnson, and Grant was uneasy as he returned to Washington to wind up the war under the direction of this new President.

The first signs were not good.

During the days immediately following Lincoln's death the government had in effect been a loose-jointed dictatorship operated by the able but completely eccentric Secretary of War, Mr. Stanton. Stanton had learned a good deal about Booth's assassination plot and he had imagined a great deal more, and blending what he knew with what he imagined, he announced (and persuaded Johnson to accept) the conviction that Jefferson Davis and the Confederate government had had an official hand in the murder conspiracy.

That this might lead Davis to the gallows was secondary. What really mattered was that it revived the worst hatreds of the war just when they were ready to subside. Americans now heard their government formally saying that the Southerners who had fought for four years had resorted to murder when the decision in the field went against them. This was not going to make it easier to work out a wholesome peace.

A secondary sign of things going wrong was the public rebuff given to General Sherman.

Sherman had sat in with Lincoln and Grant when postwar policies were discussed, and he knew Lincoln's attitude — summed up in Lincoln's homely remark, "Let 'em up easy." Soon after Lee surrendered, Sherman got a flag from Joe Johnston, in North Carolina. Johnston could do nothing else than surrender his own army; and as it happened he had just had a talk with President Davis and his cabinet, then in flight from captured Richmond, and when he met Sherman he had with him the Confederate Secretary of War, John C. Breckinridge.

Johnston and Sherman, accordingly, worked out terms that provided for the surrender, not merely of Johnston's army, but of all other armed Confederates anywhere in the South. Furthermore, they made the surrender terms in effect an outright treaty of peace, which would substantially pardon everybody for his part in the rebellion and which would also reinstall the Confederate states as regular members of a reconstituted Union.

In consenting to such terms, Sherman undoubtedly felt that he knew what Lincoln had intended. He also knew that the terms Grant gave to Lee provided, to all intents and purposes, full immunity from punishment for Lee and for every officer and man in his army. Sherman was a "hard war" man of the most determined sort, but he was as ready as Grant to let a hard war be followed by an easy peace. If Lincoln had lived it is just possible that the Sherman–Johnston–Breckinridge paper would have been accepted, although the President would have had to fight for it.

But Lincoln was in his grave and men who had the hatred which he himself had never had were running the government now. Receipt of Sherman's terms at the White House and in the War Department almost caused an explosion. Secretary Stanton was as ready to see things under the bed as any man who ever sat in the cabinet, and he immediately became convinced that Sherman was either insane or malignantly treacherous; the least Sherman would try to do, Stanton feared, would be to march his army on Washington and set up a dictatorship.

President Johnson and the rest of the cabinet did not

quite go along with this, but they did agree that Sherman had taken too much on himself in granting such sweeping terms, and it was ordered that the terms must be disavowed at once. Grant was sent down to North Carolina to tell Sherman that he could give Johnston only the terms which Grant had given Lee.

Grant handled his mission with delicacy, keeping his own part in it out of sight. Everything would have gone off smoothly if Stanton had not publicly given his dark suspicions of Sherman a full airing in Washington, denouncing this attempt to let unrepentant secessionist states take their old places in the Union, unpunished, and by implication at least accusing Sherman of the most unconscionable double-dealing.

This of course made Sherman hate Stanton all the rest of his life. Not much real harm was done there; Sherman was a fine hater and Stanton was a perfect target, and the two fitted one another. What was really harmful was the fact that this outburst stirred up old suspicions and enmities and made it harder to attain a decent peace — and thereby made it harder to protect what had been won by four years of desperate fighting.

By every gauge that can be applied, the people of the North were prepared to make peace without bitterness. Certainly the soldiers themselves wanted such a peace, and Grant and Sherman understood them and reflected their attitude perfectly. But men who held power in Washington, and wanted to go on holding that power and to get more of it if they could, would not allow that spirit to prevail if they could help it, and the outcry over what Sherman had done was an evil symptom.

Suspicion and anger were being deliberately spread

abroad, partly because designing men could gain political advantage that way, but even more because political leaders had themselves become infected with the mad passions they had created as a means of winning the war.

Their real trouble was not so much that they were selfish schemers as that they were too limited to understand that democracy cannot stand an overdose of hatred and fear. The war itself had come out of hatred and fear; now, as the war ended, they were pumping out more of the same, putting in hazard every value men had died for.

During the rest of 1865 Grant was occupied by routine, largely the routine of demobilization. Lee's surrender was just a few days old when Grant ordered recruiting stopped and made a drastic cut in military procurement. The Army of the Potomac and Sherman's army were brought back to Washington for elaborate reviews (and for the expression of a good deal of who-won-the-war rivalry which led to fist fights in practically every barroom and vacant lot in Washington). Regiment by regiment, they went home, to deposit their tattered battle flags in state capitols and to go back, as they supposed, to the old civilian routine which the war had interrupted.

Sheridan was sent to Texas with a substantial body of troops to watch the Mexican border. Napoleon III of France had installed Maximilian as puppet emperor in Mexico, taking advantage of American preoccupation with the Civil War to break the Monroe Doctrine. It was time to mend that break now, and with Sheridan and his veterans on the border, giving open encouragement and modern weapons to the Mexicans who were in the field against Maximilian, the French emperor appreciated that he had miscalculated. He withdrew his troops and left

Maximilian to his fate, which was not long in catching up with him.

Andrew Johnson, meanwhile, was beginning to see things in a different light — his own responsibilities as President, and the whole business of getting the late Confederacy back into the Union on a harmonious basis.

Under everything else, in his origins and his background, Johnson was a poor white from the deep South. As such, he hated the planter-aristocrat and wanted to see him brought down to earth; but by the same token he did not care to see the colored man elevated in his place. He had a horror of race equality and of everything that smacked of it, and when he saw that the radical Republicans' reconstruction program hinged on giving the Negro the vote, plus other privileges, he began to have second thoughts.

Unexpectedly, he ceased to breathe forth fire and slaughter, and he said no more about punishing traitors and making treason odious. Instead he adopted the Lincoln policy, a vital part of which Grant had already put into effect through his pledge that paroled Southern soldiers could not be punished.

That pledge did not go unchallenged. However the bulk of the people might feel, the Republican radicals wanted vengeance. In Johnson's own Tennessee the egregious Parson Brownlow, who had become governor through the strange gyrations of loyalist politics, was exulting that "Hell opens wide to receive the hypocrites as they come from the gibbets of the felon," and was stating his position frankly: "I am one of those at the South who believe this war was closed out two years too soon. The

Rebels have been whipped, but not whipped enough."
There were men in the North who felt the same way and
who wanted to get on with the whipping, and when Johnson suddenly offered pardon and amnesty to such Confederate leaders as would take the trouble to apply for it
they were indignant and looked for a counterstroke.

It seemed best to aim this counterstroke at General
Lee. In his own person Lee represented the Confederacy,
the Southern aristocracy and the tenacious courage and
fighting skill that had cost the lives of thousands of Northern soldiers. In midsummer of 1865 a Federal judge at
Norfolk, Virginia, called together a grand jury which indicted Lee for treason.

Lee immediately wrote to Grant asking how this
squared with the terms of surrender Grant had written at
Appomattox. With his letter, he enclosed, for Grant to
forward if he saw fit, his own application for pardon and
amnesty under the President's proclamation. (The understanding, of course, was that this application should not be
forwarded unless Grant agreed that the Appomattox
terms made an indictment for treason invalid.)

That put it all up to Grant. Lee's was the test case.

Grant acted promptly. The terms of surrender, he said,
meant exactly what they said. If the government broke
those terms it would be breaking (among other things)
the pledged word of U. S. Grant, and if that happened he
would resign his commission and take the case straight to
the country. Inasmuch as Grant at that moment enjoyed a
prestige and popularity such as Americans are willing to
confer on one of their number not oftener than two
or three times in a century, that was that. Nothing more
was ever heard about punishing Lee for treason.

Johnson made one mild protest. Nearly all Confederate officers were protected as Lee was protected, and by Grant's interpretation that protection was pretty substantial. When, asked Johnson, can these men be tried?

"Never," said Grant, "unless they violate their paroles."

3. *Voice of the People*

THEORIZING about the nature of the American Union had stopped during the war, but resumed again at the peace. In an odd sort of way people went back to the point where the argument had been dropped in 1861. This time, though, all of the theorizing was done in the North.

One theory had been held by Lincoln and was now supported by Johnson. It held that no state could possibly leave the Union under any circumstances. (It seemed logical to argue so, inasmuch as the country had just won a four-year war fought in support of the point.) Hence the former Confederate states had not actually been out of the Union at all. They had just been out of proper relationship to it, and now the relationship must be made proper again. Only a few simple things need be done to bring this about; after that, the Union would be whole again and everything would be settled.

An opposing theory, held by the radical Republicans (who, as it happened, controlled Congress) held that when the Southern states seceded they did it so successfully that they committed suicide. As states they no longer existed, and they never would exist unless the Federal government re-created them anew. The geographical area where they had been was just so much conquered territory.

As these two theories collided, in the months following Appomattox, they crossed wires with two other theories concerning the nature of the Federal government itself.

By one theory the President is dominant, within reasonable limits. He sets policy, he acts, he leads. Subject to the traditional checks and balances, he determines (for example) what ought to be done about states which have declared themselves out of the Union and are about to be declared back in it.

By the other theory Congress is dominant and the President is its agent. He executes the laws that Congress passes but he goes very little farther. If someone has to decide how the recently rebellious states can be restored to the Union, that someone is Congress.

All of these theories were loaded. The Republican party's furious drive to retain political power depended on them, and on it in turn depended the future of the country. Bound up in its intense partisan drive was a bewildering mixture of good motives and of bad ones, of lofty ideals and of predatory self-interest. The Republican party was several different things at once. It was the party that had won the war, saved the Union and freed the Negro; it was also the party that stood for high tariffs, protection for expanding industry, and give-business-what-it-wants, and some of the most forceful and acquisitive characters America ever produced stood to make incredible profits if it continued in that role. It contained idealists sincerely anxious to elevate the Negro for his own sake, and eminently practical men who planned to use the elevation of the Negro as a means of keeping the Democrats out of power. And around everything swirled the furies kicked up by the war, in an emotional tangle as hot and complex as any in American history.

At the precise center of this angry whirlwind stood U. S. Grant, who was as little fitted to discern the realities behind all of the abstractions as any man then alive. He stood there, partly because he got caught in the middle of a row between President and Congress and partly because he was by now so far above everyone else in popular imagination that the center was wherever he happened to be.

By the end of 1865 things were developing in such a way that whoever stood in the center was bound to have a very rough time of it.

Congress came back into session to find that President Johnson had stolen a march on it.

He wanted to rehabilitate the state governments in the South along what he believed were Lincoln's lines. With certain exceptions, amnesty and restoration of property were offered to all who would take an oath of loyalty. Whenever the oath-takers in a Southern state amounted to ten per cent of the 1860 electorate, these voters could form a new state government. If that government then disavowed the original ordinance of secession, ratified the constitutional amendment abolishing slavery, and repudiated the Confederate war debt, the state could return to the Union and its Senators and Representatives could sit in Congress. When the new session of Congress opened, a long queue of these reconstructed legislators was on hand, awaiting admission.

Johnson thus was denying that the states had committed

suicide and was affirming that the President dominates the Federal government. He was also reversing his old program to make treason odious; in substance, he was telling the Southerners that if they formally admitted that the Union was unbreakable and that slavery was dead they could resume their old places and no questions asked.

Congress immediately boiled over. The radical Republicans complained bitterly that this was no better than spineless appeasement of men recently in rebellion. They denounced the President for usurping power that belonged to Congress. They predicted that under this program the old coalition of Northern and Southern Democrats would be revived; that would make the Republicans a minority party, the Negro would again be at the mercy of his late masters, and effective Federal protection for the lusty industrial infants of Pennsylvania and other northern states would cease to be.

Congress refused to let the new Southern members take their seats. In effect it suspended the whole Johnson program while it considered how a new one could be framed. Simultaneously, Congress and President got into an extremely bitter contest for the support of majority opinion in the Northern states.

Johnson appeared to have public sentiment with him. The war was finished and people wanted it to stay finished. The average Northerner longed for reconciliation. Grant was generally applauded when, after a trip through Dixie, he reported that "the mass of thinking men of the South accept the present situation in good faith" and said he believed they sincerely wanted to get back into the Union as soon as they could.

But there was still the Negro, and in their fight with the

President the radical Republicans made him their favorite pawn.

Massing their idealists in the front line, they cried that these Southerners now trying to re-enter the Union were also trying to restore slavery under a different name — "serfdom, peonage or other form of compulsory labor." Freedom must be protected, emancipation must be made permanent — and for his own protection the Negro must be given the vote. No Southern state should be allowed to re-enter the Union until its colored folk had full civil rights and the franchise.

In their fight with Johnson the Republicans were greatly aided by the errors of their opposition.

Most Southern states were, as a matter of fact, passing "black codes" which were frankly designed to keep the colored man as close to slavery as possible. When radical orators complained that the Negro was in danger of being forced back into servitude they could cite chapter and verse for it. The fact that few Northern states were ready to give the Negro full citizenship was beside the point. The argument raged in an atmosphere long since poisoned — by wartime atrocity tales, by the belief that traitors ought to be hanged, by the fury Booth's insane plot had generated, by the demagogic assertion that the President was seizing a dictator's powers. Men became victims of their own emotions and lived in an era when it was not possible to carry on political debates rationally.

In addition, Andrew Johnson made his fight with Congress with an absolute minimum of skill, giving away tricks which Lincoln would have gathered in almost without effort.

The radicals won the elections in 1866, Johnson's reconstruction plan dissolved, and Congress undertook to write its own plan. Writing it, Congress made the President himself one of its targets. In its determination to assert its own prerogative it tried to destroy the President's, and in place of the Presidential dictatorship which it professed to fear it set up a Congressional dictatorship which was somewhat worse.

And Grant was in the middle of it all.

He was before long to become President of the United States, and his last two years as general gave him the worst possible training for the place. He had a defective conception of the Presidency, to begin with. When Congress replaced Johnson's reconstruction plan with its own and reduced Johnson to sheer impotence, it confirmed Grant in that defective conception and made it even more defective. In the end, it became humanly impossible for Grant to be a strong President.

Under the Republican program the South now was divided into five military districts, with a general in command of each. Until new state governments acceptable to Congress should be set up and approved, the generals commanding those districts would run things. They would also set up and supervise the machinery by which the new state governments would be established. When the Southern states did any voting, unrestricted Negro suffrage must prevail; no white man could vote unless he swore that he had always been loyal to the Union.

This quickly brought a new clash between President and Congress. Andrew Johnson liked unrestricted Negro suffrage no better than any other born-and-bred Southerner, and the army officers who must enforce this policy would, after all, be answerable to the President. Although he felt that it was his constitutional duty to try to carry out this program which Congress had enacted over his veto, he would water it down wherever he could and it was clear that he had the power to water it down quite substantially.

Congress hurried to put him in his place. It ruled that the temporary civil governments in Southern states were wholly subservient to the military commanders and through them to "the paramount authority of Congress." It then made the military commanders independent of the President by providing that no order could legally go to them except through the general commanding the army — who, in turn, was walled off by another enactment providing that he could be neither removed, suspended nor relieved unless the Senate said he could. On top of all of this Congress passed the Tenure of Office Act, asserting that no member of the President's cabinet could be removed without the Senate's consent.

Having thus removed the President from the main channels of government, Congress adjourned for the summer of 1867 and Grant found himself in charge of the whole reconstruction program.

Nobody quite knew just where Grant stood in all of this pulling and hauling. Grant himself did not know. Within the year, Congress had created the post of four-star general. Johnson had given him the job. Both Congress and President had been seeking his favor. The courtship was still going on.

Not long after Congress adjourned Johnson asked Secretary of War Stanton to resign, suspecting correctly that Stanton had been playing the radicals' game throughout. Stanton refused to resign until Congress reconvened, when it would be possible to see what the Senate had to say about it. Johnson insisted that the post was vacant, and gave it to Grant.

Grant objected strenuously, saying that "it certainly was the intention of the legislative branch of the government to place a cabinet member beyond the power of executive removal." Johnson finally talked him into taking the place on an interim basis, and for the last five months of 1867 Grant was both commanding general of the army and, in his other clothes, Secretary of War as well.

Grant tried hard to steer a middle course, but things were moving too fast to permit any neutrality to endure, and Johnson by now was well along the road toward impeachment. At the end of 1867 the Senate met and refused to consent to Stanton's dismissal. Grant then dutifully (as he supposed) surrendered the secretaryship, and Johnson flew into a mighty rage, declaring that Grant had broken his promise to hold on to the office and thereby force a court test of the Tenure of Office Act. Since Grant was touchy on any point involving his own word, this put him in a rage too, and thereafter he and Johnson were bitter enemies.

In any case, Grant's position had been hardening. Under everything else there was the traditional army officer's view that Congress is the boss. Orders may come from the executive branch but it is always Congress that passes appropriation bills, creates or abolishes army posts and functions, confirms or rejects the nominations of higher officers, declares war and ratifies treaties and in general lays down the line which the army has to follow.

This position was buttressed by Grant's deep instinct for democracy. The will of the people, he had said repeat-

edly, is the final law of the land, and all government serv-
ants from the highest to the lowest must obey it. The will
of the people, as he saw it, was to be ascertained by what
Congress said and did, Congress being the agency set up
to make that will manifest.

To a friend, in that difficult summer of 1867, Grant
wrote that "Congress has made it my duty to perform certain offices, and whilst there is an antagonism between the
executive and legislative branches of the government I
feel the same obligation to stand at my post that I did
whilst there were rebel armies in the field." The letter is
significant. Congress just then was monstrously overreach-
ing itself, but Grant could not question it. In case the issue
went to extremes he would be on the side of Congress,
simply because all his background and experience told
him that Congress must be the final authority.

The fight between Congress and President confirmed
Grant's concepts. At the same time it gave him an object
lesson about the dreadful things that can happen to a
President who fails to get along with Congress. It made it
inevitable that when he himself became President he
would provide an enduring illustration of the fact that it
can be risky to put a professional soldier in the White
House, not because the man will try to use too much authority in that position but because he will try to use too
little.

4. *Outside of Politics*

In the election of 1868 the people of the
United States made Ulysses S. Grant their President.

It was almost inevitable. Grant was the living embodi-
ment of victory. He could be relied on to protect the fruits
of victory against any possible subversion, and yet at the
same time he stood for magnanimity, understanding and
friendship with those who had lately been Confederates.
His devotion and integrity were beyond question, and it
was clear that he wanted nothing for himself except a
chance to serve his country.

Best of all, he was no politician.

If in 1868 everyone was tired of politics there was ample reason for it. For the better part of a decade the nation had been under almost unendurable tensions, and it
seemed that politics might have caused all of it, or at least
had made it all much worse than it need have been. The
unsavory political schemings of the Johnson impeachment
case had aroused genuine disgust. It was a relief, at last,
to get away from the everlasting talkers and persuaders
and promisers and turn to a decent, straightforward man
who would clean things up and take on himself the bur-
dens which everybody was tired of carrying.

When the Republican party notified him that he was
its nominee, Grant made a brief speech of which nobody
remembered anything except the final sentence — "Let us
have peace." The words fitted the public temper. Peace,
and a forgetting; sacred memories laid away in the dusk
with faded wreaths and tattered flags on half a million
soldiers' graves, and westward the old gleam on the hori-

ton again, with a famous soldier to guard what had been
won; the war was over, the old ways could be picked up
again, and the country would close the books on a tragic
chapter.

Except that the fine times which peace promised would
not appear automatically. There had been a revolution,
and the most far-reaching kind of social and economic
change had begun. Men who were tired of hating were
nevertheless plagued by hatreds when they tried to adjust
to these changes, and in all American history no more
delicate job of guidance had been required than would be
needed now. To rebuild the broken country without trying to swim against the tide of change, to make a good
synthesis out of the wildly different elements at hand —
this demanded political skill of the very highest order.
Above all other moments, this was the moment for the
politician; yet the primary appeal of the man chosen was
that he was a straightforward soldier without a politician's instinct in his whole make-up.

Probably this, too, was inevitable. Most Americans in
1868 would undoubtedly have agreed with Senator John
Sherman, who said: "The executive department of a republic like ours should be subordinate to the legislative
department. The President should obey and enforce the
laws, leaving to the people the duty of correcting any errors committed by their representatives in Congress."

This agreed perfectly with Grant's ideas. (If ever there
was a representative of the American subconscious it was
U. S. Grant.) He had said that he had no policy to enforce against the will of the people, and he had repeatedly shown that he believed that will to be expressed in
Congress. In his speech of acceptance he remarked that he

could not outline a policy for the years just ahead because new issues would arise and the public mind would change . . . "and a purely administrative officer should always be left free to execute the will of the people."

He saw himself, and the country wanted him to see himself, as a purely administrative officer. Therein lay the tragedy of his eight years in the White House, for a purely administrative officer could no more meet the problems which those eight years would bring than he could sprout wings and fly over the moon. Neither Grant nor anyone else dreamed of such a thing, but he took the office pledged in advance to failure.

The election campaign itself brought out no "issues" worth mentioning. Democratic nominee was Horatio Seymour, former governor of New York, whom good Republicans during the war had considered no better than an arrant Copperhead, and feuds long dead were revived. In the main the Republicans spent their time accusing Southerners of murdering Negroes and "loyal whites," implying that Democratic victory would practically restore the Confederacy. In turn, the Democrats accused the Republicans of favoring full social equality between the races. Grant himself made no speeches, and he was triumphantly elected. Significantly, although he had a heavy majority in the electoral college, his margin in the popular vote was not great — a majority of some 300,000 out of 5,700,000 votes cast.

Grant looked upon his election as essentially a reward by a grateful country to its foremost soldier. He had received many gifts since Appomattox, bought with funds raised by public subscriptions, and he accepted them with the most whole-souled innocence. There was precedent for such gifts: Grant was well aware of the rich rewards which the British had conferred on the Duke of Wellington. At no time did it occur to him that rich men who contributed to these funds might some day expect favors in return.

Certainly he seemed to feel that he owed the Republican party nothing in particular for the nomination it had given him, and if a few years later he was the blindest of partisans he was no partisan at all when he took office. His cabinet selections were clear proof of that. He made them as a commanding general might make appointments to his personal staff, strictly to please himself, as if he were entirely outside of the range of party politics.

Two of the most important places were handed out quite frankly as personal compliments. General John Schofield was made Secretary of War and Congressman Washburne was made Secretary of State, with the understanding in each case that the appointee would resign within a very short time and let someone else have the place. Schofield quit within a week, to be succeeded by General John A. Rawlins, on whose advice and counsel Grant had relied heavily throughout the war. Washburne served for about a month and was replaced by one of Grant's genuinely first-rate selections, Hamilton Fish of New York.

Two more appointments could be rated excellent: E. R. Hoar of Massachusetts as Attorney General and Jacob Cox of Ohio as Secretary of the Interior. (Neither man, unfortunately, was able to remain in the cabinet much longer than a year.) Secretary of the Navy was Adolph Borie, a retired Philadelphia businessman, good-natured and easy-going, whose chief contribution to the department Gideon Welles had conducted so ably was to saddle a number of good American warships with names out of Greek mythology. Postmaster General was John Creswell, of Maryland.

On one appointment Grant stubbed his toe ludicrously. For Secretary of the Treasury he named A. T. Stewart, wealthy New York merchant, on the innocent theory that so rich a businessman would save money for the country in the handling of its finances. After the Senate confirmed the nomination, however, it developed that Stewart could not legally serve because of a law providing that no man financially interested in trade or commerce could run the Treasury Department.

Grant asked the Senate to exempt Stewart from this law, and the Senate refused, stimulated to its refusal by Senator Charles Sumner, who for a variety of reasons had concluded that he was not going to get along with the new President. Stewart then offered to turn his business over to trustees to operate while he was secretary, with all profits going to charity. This too the Senate refused to agree to, and at last Stewart had to go back to New York and the Treasury position went to George S. Boutwell of Massachusetts, a conservative "hard money" man and a firm believer in rough treatment for the conquered South.

In making all of these appointments Grant consulted literally no one — neither the Republican leaders nor even, in most cases, the men whom he appointed.

The public was inclined to take this as a welcome sign that the President stood outside of politics. Actually, it was an irretrievable mistake. It killed any chance that the cabinet might be a strong political instrument binding the majority party to White House leadership. It guaranteed that Grant would never be able to enlarge the purely administrative role which he had set for himself. And it was ample notice, to the canny Republican leaders, that the new President was an utter babe in the political woods.

It was a bad time to have a political innocent in the White House, for such a one would not even be able to administer things. The tools of government often get soiled and somewhat tricky, and down at the operating level high policy can get twisted until its own father would not recognize it — as many administrators besides Grant have had to learn, to their cost. What Grant wanted was simple and good: to make a decent transition from war to peace, restoring the currency and balancing the budget and unleashing the energies of the country's expanding productive system, and at the same time to make the reunion of North and South real and lasting without sacrificing the Negro in the process.

But all of these things would have to be done through some thousands of government workers, and when Grant became President these workers were wholly dominated by a strong and far-reaching system of Congressional patronage. The average government appointee would doubtless, if left to himself, prefer to serve God rather than Mammon, but he knew perfectly well that it was Mammon who had got his job for him and who could, and without hesitation would, take it away from him if provoked. He was a drop in a stream that could never rise higher than its source, and its source lay in the political self-interest of the men who ran the Congressional patronage system.

What the Grant administration did would be changed and diluted to conform to that self-interest, and Grant's hopes for a fair and liberal reconstruction program would in the end lie at the mercy of petty unreachable men who would profit if the system were perverted into a means of winning political advantage. When he took office, Grant had the prestige and the power to force an overhaul of the entire setup, but nothing in his earlier experience told him that he would have to do it. As a general, he had always done his job independently of politics, and he would try to do the same in the White House. The very purity of his motives — his sure distaste for shabby deals and the people who made them — worked against him now. By the time he began to see how the wind was blowing it was too late, for a President who is going to bend the political system to his own will has got to do most of the bending during his first few months in office. After that, it is more likely to bend him.

In a sense, most of the important things in connection with Grant's eight years as President happened before he fairly got started. The pattern was set. Since he was not in the least stupid, he presently realized that things were going wrong, but it was never possible for him to see just how they were going wrong or what he could do to make them go right. A White House visitor who saw him about a year after he took office noticed "a puzzled pathos, as of a man with a problem before him of which he does not understand the terms."

Pathos of a different kind there was in connection with quite another White House visitor. In the spring of 1869 Robert E. Lee was in Baltimore in the interest of a projected railway line that would go up the Shenandoah Valley to Lexington, where Lee was living as president of Washington College, and while he was in Baltimore, Lee received a quiet hint that President Grant would like it if he called at the White House. Apparently Grant felt that such a visit might help to dramatize the ending of war's bitterness and the consummation of reunion.

At any rate, Lee went to the White House, and he and Grant had a chat. They had not met since Appomattox, and all that they were destined to say to each other that had any importance had long since been said. Now their meeting was brief and their talk was inconsequential. Once Grant tried a pleasantry. Referring to Lee's attempt to promote the building of a railroad, he remarked: "You and I, General, have had more to do with destroying railroads than building them." But Lee was not especially amused, and he did not smile. He was the born fighting man, and seemingly the one thing impossible for him was to exchange jests with the man who had beaten him. After a few minutes the old soldiers parted, each in his own way bound down the sunset slope.

Many people besides Lee came to the White House, once Grant was living there. Some were men of wealth and power who wanted favors from the government and believed that the way to get them was to cultivate the President; and the Grant who had so quickly spotted and suppressed the contract swindlers at Cairo seemed now to look out of duller eyes. Perhaps the man who had known such very lean years found it pleasant now to be courted by men who had made and kept much money. More possibly, it was simply harder to see clearly in the White House than it had been in an army camp, where the code of right and wrong was uncomplicated and any degree of villainy could be detected at a glance.

Perhaps it is symbolic that Grant tried to give the White

House an army camp's atmosphere. His official family of
secretaries, personal aides and so on was carried over almost en bloc from his wartime staff. He knew how a commanding general ought to act, as well as any man has ever
known, but he could not translate that knowledge to the
Presidency.

5. *The Might-Have-Beens*

It was not that Grant failed to get anything
done during his Presidency. In some ways he accomplished
a good deal, and afterward he looked back on his record
with a pride that was not altogether unjustified.

In one way or another the economic wreckage of the
war had been pretty largely cleared away. Inflation had
been stopped and the national credit had been restored.
A solid currency had been not so much restored as created
— for the nation had never before really had a uniform,
stable money system. If the real genius of America perhaps lay in its latent ability to show just how fast and far a
people could go with the miraculous processes of the industrial revolution, policies had been adopted that would
unfetter that genius. All of this had been done roughly, at
substantial cost to a great many people and at unconscionable profit to a few insiders, but at least it had been done.

Decent relations with Great Britain had at last been
made possible. Patient negotiation had led to arbitration
and final settlement, not merely of the *Alabama* claims but
of all the other points of irritation that had grown out
of the war. A second resort to arbitration had settled the

Northwest Boundary Dispute, and for the first time since it gained its independence the nation no longer had an unresolved question about any part of its borders.

Finally, the Union had been put back together again, after a fashion, and although much was said about the horrors of the reconstruction era, history had actually seen something very new and heartening — a wholly victorious government settling a four-year revolt (and an extremely bloody one, attended by great bitterness) without resorting to the gallows or the proscription list. It had tacitly admitted that there had been no treason and no traitors, and the conquered-province theory had slowly died. If blood was shed during the reconstruction period, the remarkable fact was that most of it was shed by men who stood with the victors and not with the vanquished.

In point of sober fact, American Presidents have faced smaller problems and have done much worse with them. Yet the eight years that began on March 4, 1869, were disappointing. What was done seemed then and later of less account than what was not done. Grant's record in the White House is darkened by the shadow of a few tragic might-have-beens.

Great wealth came into power with him. It was feral and hungry, the explosion of war had blown away old restraints, and the land was ripe to be plucked. America might then have had a President wise enough to see, not merely that these ambitious predators ought to be restrained somewhat, but that the bargain-counter atmosphere they brought in with them would inevitably corrupt government itself.

It might have had such a President — and yet how could it, really? For a whole generation, men of the North had learned to admire the promoter, the go-getter, the man who brought a new railroad or a new factory or a new business of any kind into existence. The great American dream always had a cash basis, and the right to enjoy absolute freedom seemed to carry with it the right to make a better living than one's father had made. Grant was never more completely true to his own time and place than in his uncritical acceptance of the men who had made much money and who proposed to make much more.

In his own field Grant had exacting standards and he knew how to apply them. He could size up generals because he was a first-rate general himself and he knew what made soldiers tick. But he could not size up rich men, because they lived in a different world. The canny common sense needed to run a Galena harness shop, or to keep an army supply system on a level keel, was not even remotely akin to the qualities possessed by the new masters of finance and industry. They operated in a different dimension, and Grant shared with his own and later generations an almost total inability to understand what they were really about.

His troubles in that respect began early and stayed late.

Two eminent New York money-makers named Jay Gould and Jim Fisk did their full share to tarnish his fame.

Gould was pure unalloyed greed, outwardly very quiet and respectable; if he had a private life aside from the pursuit of money it was doubtless impeccable. Fisk was equally rapacious, but he also had a zest for high living and it never occurred to him to restrain it. Between them, these men had all of the equipment any pirates need except cutlasses, and early in 1869, having profitably looted the Erie Railroad, they set out to make another fortune at the nation's expense by cornering the supply of gold.

Since the country had left the gold standard early in the war, speculators traded in gold as in any other commodity, buying or selling for future delivery, gambling on the swaying balance between inflation and deflation. The government owned something like one hundred million dollars' worth of gold, and each month the Secretary of the Treasury would sell a few million dollars' worth, using the proceeds to retire government bonds. If at any time the price of gold began to swing too high the secretary could bring it down by increasing the quantity of gold he offered in the market.

For Gould and Fisk, therefore, it was important to know in advance what the secretary was going to do. It would be even better if they could keep him from doing anything at all, for in that case they could drive the price up to fantastic heights and squeeze the living soul out of such persons as had sold gold on the gamble that the price would go down.

To accomplish their end, the two set out to hoodwink President Grant.

They hoodwinked him part way — enough to do a great deal of harm to the nation's economy and to Grant's good name and political fortunes, not to mention a considerable number of unlucky gold speculators who do not really deserve much sympathy.

Gould and Fisk entertained Grant, lavishly and ostentatiously, when he was in New York, and they did their best to persuade him that the crops that autumn would move to market faster and would bring better prices if the government would refuse to interfere with the play of the market place and would let the price of gold go as high as it chose to go. They took entirely into camp a feckless trader named A. R. Corbin, who was important to them because he had married Grant's sister; to Corbin they gave a small piece of the deal. As they did all of this they bought gold, and they took pains not to deny the inevitable rumor that they had influence with the President and were using it.

Grant never actually did anything for them except let himself be seen in their company. When he finally realized that something very fishy was in the wind he had Secretary Boutwell sell enough gold to break the corner, the price fell from 162 to 135, and the wild party was over. But the frenzied speculation had caused heavy loss to any number of businessmen who never bought a dollar's worth of gold in their lives, and it left many people with the suspicion that Grant had been an undercover partner in a bare-faced swindle.

Not entirely unlike this, and following hard on its heels in point of time, was the business of San Domingo.

This little Negro republic occupied two thirds of a potentially rich island in the Caribbean Sea, and it was in a chronic state of bankruptcy and revolution. When Grant became President the boss man of San Domingo was Buenaventura Baez, who was insecure and on the make. It occurred to Baez that if he could sell his country to the United States he ought to be able to make some money for himself. News of his willingness to sign a treaty of annexation got to Washington. Simultaneously, Grant learned that the United States Navy wanted Samaná Bay, at the eastern end of the island, as a coaling station.

The urge to annex San Domingo was not new. Secretary Seward had had the idea in the previous administration, although he had never tried to do anything about it because Andrew Johnson was in so much trouble that any program he sponsored was bound to fail. Now Grant picked the idea up, and as he meditated on it he concluded that it offered the opportunity of the century.

San Domingo, he believed, could easily support ten million people. Why not take it over, induce the country's recently freed slaves to move to it, let them set up three or four all-Negro states as regular members of the American Union, and thus at one stroke do justice to the Negro and also take the pesky race issue forever off the North American continent?

Few things in all his career ever moved Grant as strongly as this plan. To the end of his days he felt that it was one of the finest ideas he had ever had. Unfortunately, his attempt to put it into execution was disastrously amateurish. Instead of asking Secretary of State Fish to see what he could work out, Grant simply had his aide, Colonel Orville E. Babcock, go down to the island to arrange everything, by-passing Fish completely. In due course Babcock came back with a treaty acceptable to Baez, and Grant immediately threw all of his weight behind it.

Aside from the fact that Grant's plan for settling the Negro question in this manner was wholly visionary, the San Domingo business had a most evil odor. Baez was surrounded by utterly unscrupulous speculators, and Colonel Babcock — whose notions of the ethics of high office were not of the clearest — had got completely surrounded by them, if not actually hand in glove with them. To put it mildly, the circumstances under which the treaty had been arranged were very questionable.

When the treaty went to the Senate it fell under the immediate disapproval of haughty Charles Sumner, chair-
man of the Committee on Foreign Relations, who denounced the treaty, its origins and Babcock personally
with all the biting self-righteousness he used to pour out
on the slavery oligarchy. This made Grant and Sumner
personal enemies for life — an attack on a member of his
staff Grant always interpreted as an attack on himself —
and it also doomed the treaty. After months of wrangling
and unhappy publicity the treaty died; and what came of
it, chiefly, was a widespread impression that the President
of the United States had somehow got involved in an unsavory mess.

The gold corner and the San Domingo fiasco were sam-
ples. They indicated that Grant just was not worldly-wise
enough to see through the disguises which large-scale greed
can put on. Also, they were the tragic symptoms of a far-
reaching collapse of the standards of political integrity —
a collapse for which Grant was not in the least responsible,
but which ultimately his administration came to symbolize.

The trouble began before his election. There was for
instance the matter of Crédit Mobilier.

Crédit Mobilier was a construction company which powerful insiders in the heavily subsidized Union Pacific Railroad Company had organized. It built the railroad, and the
insiders who owned it were in a position to approve the
charges which it levied, and as a result it was fantastically
profitable. In 1868 a competent authority estimated that
that year's dividends — in cash, in bonds and in stock —
amounted to better than 340 per cent of the total par value
of the stock on which the dividends were declared.

There was danger, of course, that Congress might some day look into all of this, and so one of the insiders in Crédit Mobilier, a gentleman named Oakes Ames, himself by happy chance a member of Congress, took a hundred and sixty shares of this fabulous stock and passed them around in Congress where they would do the most good. Some highly respectable legislators were on his list, and a gaudy time they had a bit later explaining how they had been able to hold this stock with no harm to their integrity.

For the whole story came out, of course, in the end. It came out just as Grant's first term was ending, so that although the entire business had been cooked up and put over before Grant became President, the Crédit Mobilier scandal came to rest right in the middle of his administration's record.

Yet the real measure of Grant's evil fortune was not simply that he was thus stained by other men's sins. Here was a man who deeply believed that Congress expressed the will of the people and must fix the policies that the President would administer; and the Congress to which he was thus turning over so much of his own responsibility was not only capable of glossing over its own venality but was wholly incapable of understanding that the real swindle lay in the fact that Crédit Mobilier existed at all.

If leaders in Congress could be like that, there would be men in the government departments and agencies who could be much worse. Civil service as it then existed was, as Secretary of the Interior Cox remarked, "little better than a nuisance." The spoils system was in full bloom, and it was operated by politicians whose ethical standards were those of Crédit Mobilier. Corruption spread across the board — in the customs offices, in the tax bureaus, in the land offices and the Indian agencies and everywhere else. Mark Twain wrote sardonically that a tax agent showed him how to dodge his income tax payments, and said that he swore to lies and frauds "until my soul was coated inches and inches thick with perjury and my self-respect gone forever and ever." But, added the satirist, what of it? — "It is nothing more than thousands of the richest and proudest and most respected, honored and courted men in America do every year."

It was not peculiar to the Federal government. The appalling Tweed Ring scandal in New York City broke just at this time, with its revelation of unblushing thefts on an almost inconceivable scale. The carpetbag governments of the supposedly reconstructed Southern states were monuments of waste and crookedness — and yet, on the whole, their record was matched (except for the picturesque trimmings) by the records of old established state governments in the North. It was as if government everywhere, tailored to the measure of a smaller and less complicated country, and then cracked by the strain of war, had become completely unable to cope with commercial and industrial rapacity.

Something could have been done about it, of course. As a first step, the civil service system could have been put on a rational basis. There was developing a strong demand that this be done, and Grant went along with it. In the spring of 1871 Congress authorized him to provide rules and regulations to promote efficiency and honesty in the government service, and Grant set up a commission under the chairmanship of George William Curtis. This commission presently recommended a set of rules which would have brought about a real merit system. In December of that year Grant sent up a special message, asking Congress to vote the money and the authority to put the system into operation.

It could have been done. The patronage system was deeply entrenched, but the cost of it was all too visible and people had grown very tired of it. Republican leaders of substantial prestige were ready to help, for "reform" was a popular issue. A President prepared to wage a dogged, determined fight could have put it over.

But although he was a dogged and determined fighter, Grant could not wage such a fight on this issue — because the Congressional leaders who were his chief supporters were dead set against it. Such stalwarts as Senators Roscoe Conkling of New York, Oliver P. Morton of Indiana and Simon Cameron of Pennsylvania, not to mention the ineffable Ben Butler in the House, took up arms against the measure. They had gone along with Grant on the San Domingo deal, they had backed his reconstruction measures, they were in fact the men who really controlled administration policy; how could he go against them? He had made, in short, the cardinal mistake which comes most naturally to the amateur in the White House: perceiving finally that a good part of politics is the art of making compromises, he had made his compromises with the wrong men, on the wrong issues, for the wrong reasons. Now they had him.

In the end Congress refused to do anything substantial for civil service reform and Grant failed to insist on it, and he lost the support of the very Republicans he needed most — men like Jacob Cox (out of the cabinet, by now), Carl Schurz, Charles Francis Adams, Charles Sumner: men who took ideals into politics with them, and who if they were determined to protect the Negro while rebuilding the Union based their determination on principle rather than on a desire for shoddy political advantage.

By the end of Grant's first term the wing of the Republican party that followed such leaders was permanently in opposition. Grant probably would have lost the 1872 election, except that his opponents made a profound tactical blunder.

The reform Republicans and the Democrats made book: they would unite on a platform and on a candidate, and then they would throw Grant and the bitter-end radical Republicans out of office and set up an administration pledged to a more moderate reconstruction policy, to full civil service reform and to a lower tariff — for the connection between the general atmosphere of complacent corruption and big industry's insistence on tariff protection had begun to dawn on them.

Having agreed on all of this, the dissident Republicans, by a superhuman feat of miscalculation, persuaded the Democrats to accept Horace Greeley as the Presidential nominee.

Greeley was a good and humane man, and in the Republican party he spoke for the idealism and sanity which had originally stood behind Grant. But his ideas on civil service and tariff reform were no better than Grant's, and for a full generation all Democrats had been brought up to detest him. In addition, he was a born eccentric, with something faintly comic about him, and it was really hard to argue that he would make an adequate President. So the voters rejected him and Grant had his second term — under conditions which meant that the troubles of his first term would be multiplied.

6. *The Unsolved Problem*

EVERYTHING HAD BEGUN with the race problem and everything finally turned on it. The move for Southern independence was dead and Negro slavery had vanished, but the race problem had been at the bottom of both and the race problem was vividly and furiously alive.

About this problem there had grown up, in the South and in the North as well, a bewildering tangle of hopes, prejudices, fears, misunderstandings and enmities. Groping their way, men still gripped by the emotions of war tried to find some sort of solution — and, as they tried, were misled by appeals to terror and anger rather than to intelligence.

There was no clear-cut choice between justice and injustice, and anyway most people who were looking for justice also had an eye open for political advantage. Lofty idealism walked arm in arm with the most brutal self-seeking.

Perhaps it was simply impossible for fallible human beings to reach a solution to the problem in the 1870's. Yet more might have been done than actually was done. The trouble was not so much that the race problem finally went unsolved as that in the end there was agreement not to try to solve it.

Grant approached reconstruction with several advantages, including instinctive fairness and humanity. He did not believe in punishing the South, he wanted the Union restored as soon as possible, and he believed that the Negro must be fully protected in his new freedom. These goals were simple, but the road to them was full of extraordinary complexities.

Facing a terrible difficulty — the need to adjust to the loss of its basic social and economic institution, and the requirement that it keep its hands off while the Negro took his first inexpert steps on the road to freedom — the South played its cards very badly. It passed laws in which Grant and many others saw a thinly veiled attempt to restore slavery under another name. The South had refused to accept the electoral verdict of 1860; now it was argued (by men with throats of brass) that it was refusing to accept the verdict of war.

This played directly and disastrously into the hands of the least scrupulous and least responsible men in the North — the men who, whether or not they honestly cared what happened to the Negro, were delighted to use him as a means of getting and keeping political power, accompanied on occasion by rich graft and perquisites.

Grant was not able to keep up with the intricacies of the situation. It appeared that the Negro's rights would be insecure unless he had the vote, so universal Negro suffrage was decreed. It proved quite simple for Southerners to keep the Negro from the polls by fraud and by violence, and so Federal troops were called on. When Southerners reacted defiantly to such measures, sterner measures were adopted. Step by step, repression took the place of reconciliation, and the Negro's rights were lost to view in the struggle to break the will of the former

Confederates. Grant lacked the political skill to keep from being maneuvered into a position where the most extreme policy was his policy, and where the most violent partisans claimed him as their leader.

It seemed to Grant all-important that the colored man must not be thrown to the wolves in the reconstruction of the Union. Most other Republicans saw it the same way, but neither the "reform" wing of the party nor the average Northern voter had any taste for reconstruction governments kept in office only by the bayonets of regular troops and the progressive disfranchisement of the white population. Men like Schurz and even Sumner could accept the need for flexibility, compromise, and a willingness to see the problem otherwise than (both literally and figuratively) in terms of unrelieved blacks and whites.

Grant really belonged with this group. Yet the gulf between him and the moderate Republican leaders had become too wide to cross. Grant's personal fight with Sumner, arising largely from the San Domingo deal, probably had a good deal to do with it. From it Grant acquired a bitter contempt for what he considered the holier-than-thou reformers — "the narrow-headed men," as he called them, whose eyes were so close together that "they can look out of the same gimlet hole without winking." The moderates had led in the fight for civil service reform, they had tried to keep Grant from having a second term, they opposed the high-tariff people who gave Grant such unwavering support — and, altogether, they had that hateful characteristic in regard to gimlet holes, and Grant could not work with them.

With the extremists he could work; with them, finally,

he had to work. They knew full well how to take his inflexible determination that the verdict of the war was not to be reversed in the process of reconstruction, and use it to their own advantage. When infuriated Southerners took up arms to maintain white supremacy, these leaders could tell Grant that this simply proved that the men who had recently tried to destroy the government were at it again. Such villains were Democrats, naturally; and ex-Democrat Grant was informed on all sides that during the war the Northern Democrats had been the Confederacy's disloyal accomplices. If the Democrats regained control in the South they and the Northern Democrats would soon be running the Federal government, and that would undo victory itself.

There could be no retreat. The reconstruction program would have to get stiffer and stiffer — until, at last, it broke. The tragedy was that when it did break, the attempt to solve the race problem would die for many years to come.

Always the instinct had been to ignore the problem rather than to try to solve it.

That instinct had led the slavocracy before the war to glorify slavery as a positive good which must not be touched, even if destruction of the Union were the price of its untouchability. The same instinct made Lincoln and men like him grope wistfully for some scheme of colonization to get colored people entirely out of the country. It had caused Grant himself to espouse the San Domingo treaty. In a hazy way it had even led the extreme abolitionists to adopt the conquered-province theory, as if the race problem might look a little better, somehow, if it were just turned upside down.

But no effort at evasion would do. The two races lived side by side in one community and they always would, and sooner or later the nation would have to turn that fact into something better than a source of hatred, oppression and bloodshed. Victory in the Civil War had made a solution even more imperative, for it had infinitely broadened the category of American citizenship and the meaning of the American experiment. Nobody quite meant it that way, but ultimately it had committed the nation to a working belief in the brotherhood of man.

This probably was a little too much to swallow at one gulp, in the 1870's or at any other time. Perhaps the real trouble with the reconstruction era was that it called on everybody to rise above his own limitations and nobody was quite up to it.

Grant did his best, and to the bitter end he stood for the belief that the problem at least had to be grappled with. If his program for reconstruction was finally handled wrongly, by bad people, for unworthy motives, he at least had tried to point it in the right direction. The real evil of the reconstruction era lies in what did not happen rather than in what did.

Grant had been the most popular man in America when he entered the White House, and he was a great distance from being the most popular when at last he left it.

Civil service reform had been wholly abandoned. In 1874 Grant told Congress that if it did not in that session pass effective civil service legislation he would assume that the country simply did not want any. Congress took no action, and Grant said no more about it. He had come to believe that the whole argument was synthetic, and he remarked that "there is a good deal of cant about civil service reform which throws doubt upon the sincerity of the whole movement."

Financial panic came in 1873, with the great banking house of Jay Cooke and Company closing its doors. Other banks followed suit, business firms did likewise, and there was a sharp depression. Pressure mounted for currency inflation, but Grant maintained his stand for sound money, vetoing a greenback bill that rode through Congress on a wave of public discontent. (The veto did nothing to add to Grant's popularity.) Times continued bad, and people grew tired of government for the benefit of the rich and powerful. Mixed with the hoarse conflicting demands for unrestricted Negro suffrage and for full reenfranchisement of Southern whites came strident new voices — of greenbackers and of grangers and of all the economically oppressed, bitter complaints against monopoly and high finance, demands for broader rights for labor and the farmer. If big business was to complain during later generations about popular distrust and antagonism, the foundation for it all was now being laid.

The scandals grew worse, until they seemed almost universal. Secretary of War William W. Belknap was involved in graft at army posts on the frontier. Speaker of the House James G. Blaine, presently to be a plumed knight in campaign oratory and a continental liar in campaign doggerel, was mixed up in an unsavory railroad deal which he could never quite explain away. Grant's own Colonel Babcock was indicted for his connection with a plundering whiskey ring in the Midwest.

The political house rocked, and the Butlers and the Camerons and the Conklings and others who really ran the show replied with the only tactic they could think of: they centered attention on "terrorism" in the South, where unrepentant Confederates (as they insisted) were murdering colored folk by platoons. If they themselves were accused of sheltering corruption, they replied that they were defending the ideals for which heroic Union soldiers had died at Gettysburg and Chattanooga. This operation became known as "waving the bloody shirt," and the worse the political outlook became the more desperately the shirt was waved.

Grant was helpless. None of the great qualities that had served him so well during the war was of any use now. The very simplicity of his nature, which made him cut problems down to a few fundamentals, was a handle for the extremists to grip while they struggled to preserve their power.

Grant believed that the most important single issue was the reconstruction program. He believed that the sacred heart of that program lay in the effort to protect the Negro in his new freedom. He believed too (and with a good deal of reason) that the Negro would infallibly be trodden back down into second-class citizenship or worse unless the strong arm of the Federal government protected him.

So far, so good: both hard fact and clear logic could support this position. Yet the old political error was all-crippling, now. The men who supported Grant on this stand were the men who definitely were not in politics for their health, and with such defenders the colored man was in a dire fix. These men had succeeded in hiding Grant's own decent integrity behind their own devious desire to retain political power. Instead of protecting the Negro in his new freedom they had made the North very tired of the whole business, so that the nation was in a mood to cry: For Heaven's sake, sweep the whole mess under the rug if you can't do anything else, but at least get it out of sight so we can go on about our ordinary business!

. . . The extremists wanted to nominate Grant for a third term, but it just could not be done. The party finally nominated the ultrarespectable Rutherford B. Hayes, three times governor of Ohio and possessor of a good war record. The Democrats named the equally respectable Samuel J. Tilden of New York, a corporation lawyer who had helped to overthrow the Tweed Ring. In the campaign the Democrats talked about hard times and the Republicans flourished the bloody shirt, and Tilden got a substantial majority of the votes.

He did not get into the White House, however. Scenting an exceptionally close finish in the electoral college, the Republicans got their final partisan advantage out of the carpetbag regimes in the South, and by a sequence of the most unvarnished frauds managed to count the votes of Louisiana and Florida for Hayes, giving him the election by 185 electoral votes to 184. They had stolen the election and everybody knew it, and for a time it almost looked as if the Civil War might start up over again.

But the country had had one experience with going to war over an unpleasant election result, and that one was more than enough. Also with U. S. Grant in the White House it was quite certain that all of the armed might of the Federal government would be brought down hard on anyone who tried to take up arms.

Eventually, there was an adjustment.

The Democrats agreed to let Hayes have the place. In

return, by a quiet but effective understanding, the new administration pulled Federal troops out of the South, the last of carpetbagism died forever, the colored man discovered where his place was and dutifully got into it, and the reconstruction program was over.

And U. S. Grant was a private citizen again.

7. *If It Takes All Summer*

HE HAD HAD about all that any American can get — the four stars of a general and two terms in the White House, plus enough gifts, testimonials and public functions to crowd half a dozen lifetimes — and somehow most of it had been a cloak for ill fortune. A shadow lay across his fame. To millions of people his name had come to mean everything that he himself was not, as if the Whiskey Ring and the bloody shirt carried a deeper meaning than Vicksburg and Appomattox.

And then, at the very last, after a few empty years that meant nothing in particular, fate gave him good fortune in the disguise of absolute and final catastrophe. He lost all of his money and he was sentenced to die by slow torture; and through these things he once again found a task he could do superlatively well, and his old virtues of courage and determination blazed up to light his way down the valley of final shadows.

Leaving the White House in 1877, Grant was on his own for the first time since Governor Yates asked him to help with the muster of the Illinois volunteers, sixteen years earlier.

Ever since his Ohio boyhood he had liked to travel, and now he gratified that liking to the full. He started off on a transatlantic cruise, taking ship from Philadelphia, accompanied down Delaware Bay by whistle-tooting tugs and excursion steamers, and he wandered from England to the Continent and back to England again in an erratic zigzag without goal or program. He was received by kings and by parliaments, and he was looked at by millions of ordinary folk. He received the freedom of various cities and he listened to any number of addresses of welcome. And finally he went all the way around the world, and he did not get back to America until the autumn of 1879. His world tour had lasted a little less than two and one half years. Incidentally, it had consumed most of his cash savings.

It was a planless sort of wandering, because in truth Grant was at a loose end. There is seldom anything very significant for an ex-President of the United States to do, and it was harder for Grant than for most of that select breed to find an occupation for himself. Without plan or prospects, he simply drifted about the world as an unattached famous personage.

The years had changed him a little, and his photographs show it. There is a lean hard look on the face that was photographed during the war, as if the man behind the face knew exactly where he was going and could not be kept from getting there. The civilian in frock coat and top hat visible in the pictures made a dozen years later is a little stouter and a little softer, better groomed and cared for but somehow slightly at a loss, with the look of a man who does not quite know where he has been. It was noted on the world tour that the Grant who had once disliked ceremony and adulation seemed to get genuine pleasure out of them. It was as if the medals and speeches and cheering crowds gave him a welcome reassurance; and yet in the old days, even when everything was going very badly, this man had never needed reassurance.

No matter. He came back to America, landing in San Francisco, and they made a big occasion out of it, with flags tossed into the wind and a committee of eminent citizens to meet his ship. (He had left this city a quarter century earlier, out of the army and on his uppers, lacking the price of a steamship ticket to New York.) As he traveled east there were whistle-stop receptions of high and low degree, and when he reached Chicago the city was all bunting and cheers and there was a big parade, with Phil Sheridan out of the past riding at the head of it and any number of old soldiers in the ranks.

People seemed honestly glad to see him again. A little perspective had been gained during his years out of office, and it could be seen that he had given the country ever so much more than the partisan highbinders had been able to take away. Yet the welcomes were not entirely spontaneous, for the Republican old guard was helping to pump them up. If his popularity revived enough, he might have a third term. The old guard was not happy with President Hayes. The lush pickings of the reconstruction era were gone and reform was the word, and it would be nice to turn the clock back a decade.

Grant seemed willing. He had always had a slightly fatalistic attitude toward promotion, from the day when he first got a brevet in Mexico, and from beginning to end the step from general to President had seemed to him to be essentially a promotion, differing only in degree from the step from colonel to brigadier. Besides, he had nothing to do these days. By the time the Republican convention of 1880 met, a full-scale Grant boom was under way.

The attempt was hopeless. When the balloting began Grant had a plurality but his managers could never turn it into a majority, and after a long deadlock the nomination at last went to James A. Garfield. Garfield went on to become President, and the long row over reform produced an infuriated place-seeker who killed him after he had been in office a few months; and private citizen Grant was still trying to find a proper niche for himself in civilian life.

Inevitably, he drifted to New York. (Galena he had tried again, but somehow his horizons had changed and the place was no longer quite wide enough for him.) He tried this and that and nothing quite panned out, and at last he went into business with a Wall Street broker named Ferdinand Ward, with whom his elder sons had had some profitable dealings. The investment firm of Grant and Ward came into being, and into it Grant put all of his capital, together with a hundred and fifty thousand dollars borrowed from William K. Vanderbilt.

It seemed, for a time, that solid prosperity had been attained, and as far as Grant knew he was a comparatively wealthy man, partner in a well-established business.

Then came disaster.

Ward was no more a fit person to lead Grant through the business world than Ben Butler had been fit to lead him in the world of politics; in each case, a trickster used the general's name and confidence for his own ends. The firm of Grant and Ward went broke with startling suddenness, in the middle of 1884, and in the course of one day Grant learned that every last cent he owned (plus all the money he had borrowed) was gone forever and that his partner was nothing more than a swindler.

The partnership was bankrupt for a prodigious sum, a great deal of which had been lost by people who had invested because they trusted the great name of Grant; and the man whose one solid pride had always been in his own good name was compelled to see, at last, how that name had been sullied and misused by men to whom he had given his trust.

His own financial pinch was acute. To a friend, just after he got the bad news, Grant summed it up: "When I went down town this morning I thought I was worth a great deal of money, but now I don't know that I have a dollar." Actually, he was hard pressed for ordinary housekeeping money. A friend loaned him a thousand dollars to tide him over; and one day a letter came from a total stranger, enclosing five hundred dollars with a note saying that this was a payment on account "for my share of services ending April 1, 1865."

That was heart-warming, but the fact remained that the disaster was all-embracing. Grant had no money, the taint of the bucket shop hung over him, and he seemed no more able now to provide for his family than he had been back in the hardscrabble days in Missouri.

And it was imperative that he think about providing for his family, because in the middle of all of this misfortune Grant learned that he had cancer of the throat.

So now the end of the road was nearly in view. It had been a long strange road, winding across mid-America from dark valley to mountain peak, leading through battle smoke and the wild uproar of combat to an oath taken in front of the capitol and a long view of America through White House windows. In it there had been tremendous success and great fame and bewildering tragedy, and now it was going to end this way — with the mocking ghost of old Jesse Grant somewhere in the background, shaking his head and repeating his ancient complaint that West Point had spoiled his oldest son for business.

There was not much of the road left, but there was room in it for one more fight, and it was a fight Grant could win. The man who had taken many cities would at last fight a battle with his own spirit, and with death at his elbow and pain rising to its unendurable crescendo he would put despair and discouragement under his feet and do the last job there was for him to do . . . and make his exit, at last, like a victor.

The job itself was simple enough. Grant would write his memoirs.

The country was re-examining its Civil War experience, and books by men who had fought in the war were in demand. As the most famous old soldier of all, Grant would find a ready market, and his memoirs would make a modest fortune and leave a comfortable estate for his family — if he could just get them written. He was not exactly a writing man by nature, although he did own the priceless ability to express himself very clearly in simple language. He was popularly supposed to be rather inarticulate, as if he were intellectually muscle-bound.

But he had had great years and he had had time to sort out his thoughts about them, and in any case what mattered now was that life had once more — after so long a time — given him the kind of challenge that he could meet. Courage and determination were of use to him now, for life was suddenly reduced to its elementals, and in a way he was back where he had been when he wrote: "I propose to fight it out on this line if it takes all summer."

It took more than all summer, as it turned out. It took all the rest of Grant's life, which lasted a little more than a year, so that he finished his book a scant day or two before he died, and the pages of his original manuscript are eloquent in a way Grant did not intend, for they tell their own story of his last battle.

In the beginning these pages are very neat, with regular lines of inked script marching across good paper, corrections and interlineations carefully made in the proper order, penmanship regular and easily legible. The corrections show a man rereading what he had written, striking things out here and there, looking for words and phrases that would more exactly express his thoughts, sometimes knocking out whole paragraphs — and, occasionally, feeling apparently that after all these years some of his judgments might as well be withheld from print.

But toward the last, physical weakness and sheer agony begin to leave their unmistakable traces. (Grant might have died sooner, if he had permitted it, and at times his doctors resorted to elaborate expedients to keep him alive. Every added day of life was an added day of torture, and death now was a friend; but he had to live until he got this job done . . . *if it takes all summer*.) The rough paper of a schoolboy's tablet replaces the smooth bond used earlier, and instead of pen and ink the general is using a pencil, and at times the writing becomes a desperate scrawl, very hard to decipher.

You can see him, no longer able to sit at a desk, holding

a scratch-pad in his lap, driving away at it with gripped pencil. There are hardly any more corrections; now the man is fighting to get the job done while the light lasts, and there is no time for trimming and polishing. The narrative no longer flows in smooth, well-thought order. From page to page the subject changes abruptly, as if the writer wants to get his ideas down and trust his editor to put things into sequence.

Toward the very last the writing becomes skeletonized, as if pain and the rising mist made it impossible to get every word in. Yet he would keep at it, he would finish this job in spite of everything, and if at times successive pages become no better than a collection of unrelated notes for insertion at different places in the narrative, there is no mere gibberish and confusion. Down to the very end Grant knew just what he wanted to say and, very largely, how he wanted to say it, but as he fought off unimaginable pain he left a little more to his editor.

Three times he scribbled off a section under the heading "Conclusion." (In the published book, the chapter so marked is a blend of the three versions. It appears that Grant did have a very able editor. Be it noted, though, that no part of his book was ghostwritten.) The race problem bothered him, and at different times he wrote: "I do not know now how it is to terminate . . . problem yet to be solved as to how two races will get along together in future . . . our duty to inflict no further wrong on the Negro." Those last ten words, written in the hour of the last backward glance, when every written word was bought at the price of endured agony, contain the key to everything he was driving at in the reconstruction program.

One of the final pages, curiously, is half covered with doodles: a flat-roofed house, a series of squares and triangles, a little aimless crosshatching. Time might be running out, but U. S. Grant was not going to be rushed out of all countenance. After all, this was the general who sat on a stump and casually whittled during the great battle of the Wilderness.

Toward the end his mind roamed back through many battles, and the last pages are an unclassified set of paragraphs meant to be inserted somewhere earlier: a critique of what Thomas did at Nashville, some notes on Chattanooga, a rehash of Grant's old plan to capture Mobile and how Halleck blocked it. On the back of the very last page is a two-sentence reference to the way Colonel Joshua Chamberlain of the 20th Maine was wounded in action at Petersburg, and how for his valor Grant made him a brigadier general on the spot. Then, having made sure that he had paid proper tribute to a brave soldier, Grant stopped writing. Within forty-eight hours he was dead — on July 23, 1885.

What he had set out to do, Grant had done. He wrote his story and he climbed back out of poverty, and he left a decent estate for his family when he died. (He had licked the eternal world of the Jesse Grants, after all.) But while he was doing all of this, Grant did a great deal more. Going back along the old road he somehow found himself, and a good many of the things that had stuck to him during the might-have-been years seem to have scaled off.

For although the manuscript pages which Grant left may show the most excruciating physical suffering, the book itself has a glow and a shine that could only come from

a contented spirit. In its essence, the book is a record of
what Grant saw when he looked back on things from his
deathbed, and apparently what he saw was very good.

. . . the old days in Ohio, when the land was open and
the world was young, and a boy could ride a horse down
an infinite sandy road with a dapple of sunlight and
shadow resting on his shoulders; Mexico, where youth had
been a stack of golden coins to be spent prodigally amid
the dangers and romance of a marvelous drowsy land of
beauty and flowers; the West Coast, with green forests and
white surf and blue sea making an enchantment that no
memory of failure or malice could spoil; Missouri and
Illinois before the war, where life had been good even
when it was dark and hard, and where tough times had
brought happiness because Julia and the children were
there and everything one did was done for them and
with them.

And always the army: not the thin companies of regulars at lonely frontier posts, but the army that was a nation on the march — endless columns of men in faded blue
swaying forward on the eternal road, glimpsed like figures
in a red mist, always going toward some unseen goal that
could neither be attained nor given up . . .

All of this was what could be seen when Grant looked
back from the final bend in the road: his own life, and
the national life which it symbolized, tragedy touched by
remembered moments of hope. Victory and death were
forever bound together; and over all of it, the sunlight on
a broad land brimming over with life and forever on
the move.

A Note on the Sources

ALTHOUGH few Americans have been written about more than Ulysses S. Grant, a really comprehensive biography of the man does not exist. The reader who wants to study Grant in detail must go to many books by many authors.

The best place to begin is with the general himself; of all the men who wrote about U. S. Grant it was he himself who did the best job. His *Personal Memoirs* (1885–1886) leaves various things untold and occasionally shows a confused memory in operation, but it is as completely readable a work as the Civil War produced.

For Grant's life prior to the Civil War, by all odds the best work is Lloyd Lewis's *Captain Sam Grant* (1950). It is one of the tragedies of American literature that Lewis did not live to complete the definitive biography of which this was to have been the first volume. Unlike so many men who wrote about Grant, Lewis really understood him.

Of the older biographies, William Conant Church's *Ulysses S. Grant and the Period of National Preservation and Reconstruction* (1897) has a good deal of informative detail, as does Hamlin Garland's *Ulysses S. Grant: His Life and Character*

(1898). James G. Wilson's *General Grant* (1897) is readable, if uncritical; also readable, although subject to bias, is *The Life of Ulysses S. Grant* by Charles A. Dana and James H. Wilson (1868). There is still more bias, and less professional competence, in Adam Badeau's *Military History of Ulysses S. Grant* (1868).

Not to be overlooked for the revealing if sometimes sketchy light they throw on Grant's own viewpoints are *General Grant's Letters to a Friend, 1861–1880,* edited by James Grant Wilson (1897); *Letters of Ulysses S. Grant to His Father and Youngest Sister,* edited by Jesse Grant Cramer (1912); and *Ulysses S. Grant: Conversations and Unpublished Letters* by M. J. Cramer (1897). John Russell Young's *Around the World with General Grant* (1897) shows the general expressing himself freely on a wide variety of subjects.

In assessing Grant as a soldier, a balance is at last beginning to be struck between the wildly uncritical acclaim of the immediate postwar years and the equally uncritical Grant-is-a-stupid-butcher line of more recent years.

Reappraisals by British critics are to be found in *The Generalship of Ulysses S. Grant* by J. F. C. Fuller (1929), and *The Military Genius of Abraham Lincoln* by Colin R. Ballard (1926). T. Harry Williams's excellent *Lincoln and His Generals* (1952) can profitably be read with these. Another good modern study, not so much of Grant individually as of the whole command problem confronting the Federals in the Civil War, is the still incomplete *Lincoln Finds a General* of Kenneth P. Williams (1949–1952). Lloyd Lewis's *Sherman: Fighting Prophet* (1932) tells nearly as much about Grant as it does about Sherman, and there is a first-rate analysis of the general's development in A. L. Conger's *The Rise of U. S. Grant* (1931).

Books by Grant's contemporaries which present interesting pictures of Grant during the war are almost innumerable. Particularly recommended are *Personal Recollections* by Grenville M. Dodge (1902); *Campaigning with Grant* by Horace Porter (1897); *Recollections of the Civil War* by Charles A. Dana

(1899); *Under the Old Flag* by James H. Wilson (1902); *Military Reminiscences of the Civil War* by Jacob D. Cox (1900); and *Personal Memoirs of John H. Brinton, Major and Surgeon, 1861–1865* (1914).

The relationship between Grant and General George H. Thomas was occasionally somewhat strained, and a study of it can be enlightening. An account by a contemporary is *The Life of General George H. Thomas* by Thomas B. Van Horne (1882); more recent is Richard O'Connor's *Thomas: Rock of Chickamauga* (1948).

Extremely valuable for the light they throw on the war as a whole and, very often, on Grant specifically, are the excellent *Papers* of the Military Historical Society of Massachusetts, edited by Theodore Dwight (1895). It probably should go without saying that the "Battles and Leaders" series (1884–1887) contains much material on Grant and his campaigns.

The best studies of Grant in the White House are two modern works: Allan Nevins's *Hamilton Fish: The Inner History of the Grant Administration* (1936); and William B. Hesseltine's *Ulysses S. Grant: Politician* (1935).

INDEX

Index